KT-218-170

EDINBURGH
the BEST!
THE ONE TRUE GUIDE

Peter Irvine
and
Keith Davidson

HarperCollins*Publishers*

HarperCollins Publishers
Westerhill Road, Bishopbriggs, Glasgow G64 2QT

www.**fire**and**water**.com

First published 1998
This updated edition 2000

Reprint 10 9 8 7 6 5 4 3 2 1 0

© Peter Irvine, 1998, 1999, 2000

Photographs: page 14 (© Malmaison), page 28 (© The Point), page 84
(© Keith Hunter), page 66 (© Valvona & Crolla), page 89 and section
headings (© Stephen Whitehorne), page 124 (© Borthwick Castle)

ISBN 0 00 472464-X

A catalogue record for this book is available from the British Library

All rights reserved

Printed in Italy by Amadeus S.p.A.

CONTENTS

WHERE TO DRINK

WHERE TO GO IN TOWN

WHERE TO GO OUT OF TOWN

The telephone code for Edinburgh is 0131

INTRODUCTION

Welcome to the first edition of the new millennium of this city handbook extracted and updated from *Scotland the Best!* which, now in its fifth edition, has proven to be the most popular independent guide to our incredible country. Coming out every two years, it's the one the Scots use themselves, an insider guide written like this one by people who know and love their subject. Edinburgh is a big subject: here it has been reduced and condensed so that only the good information is included. You should need no other guide, but please let us know what you think – we thrive on feedback.

As you become familiar with *Edinburgh the Best!*, you will see that it is not quite like other guides. It doesn't give you lots of orientation information (it assumes you can negotiate your own arrival and can follow universal rules for survival in a new city) and you may need to consult a proper map (available free along with loads of other bumf from the Tourist Information Centres at the airport and near Waverley Station) since our maps are very diagrammatic. What it does give you in a broad range of categories is the best of what Edinburgh (and its immediate area) has to offer. We are highly selective and do not give all the options – only the best places. This includes the obvious, like the Castle, as well as the obscure, but nowhere is listed just because it's there – if it's mediocre, we ignore it. So, we're not too horrible about anyone – this is a positive book.

Although the selection process is undertaken by us, many people are consulted before choices are made and everywhere has been visited and sampled. We hope we are saving you the bother of having a less than satisfactory experience and we stand by all our recommendations. But nobody pays for inclusion, there are no ads, no subscriptions and no sponsorship. We do not employ a rigid set of standards and we tolerate idiosyncrasy because we'd rather have integrity and authenticity than mere amenity. Quality and attitude are what we recognize and want to bring to your attention. Service and atmosphere, attention to detail and value for money are all evaluated in making our decisions. This guide is written for you – not them – and not the 'industry'.

We want you to know that Edinburgh is one of the best cities on earth, and getting better all the time.

Enjoy it!

A DECLARATION OF FALLIBILITY

This guide is 'true', but it may not always be absolutely accurate. Since this may seem like a contradiction in terms, I should explain. *Edinburgh the Best!* is a handbook of information about all the 'best' places in Edinburgh. 'Best', you will understand, is a subjective term; it means 'best' according to what we think. Needless to say, there seem to be a lot of readers who agree with this judgement, and even if you don't you may see that I and my associates have gone to some efforts to reach our assertions. It's intended to be obvious that we are conveying opinions and impressions. They're true because the motives are true; we believe in what we are saying. We take no bribes and we have no vested interest in any of the places recommended, other than that we do talk things up and shamelessly proclaim the places we like or admire.

We hope it's plain where the facts end and the opinions begin. In guidebooks this is not always the case. However, it's with 'the facts' that inconsistencies may appear. We try to give accurate and clear directions explaining how to find a place and basic details that might be useful. This information is gleaned from a variety of sources and may be supplied by the establishment concerned. We do try to verify everything usually by visiting but things change and since nowhere we recommend has solicited their inclusion – we don't run copy past them – inaccuracies may occur. We hope that there aren't any, or many, but we may not find out until you let us know. We'd appreciate it if you would, so we can fix it for the next edition.

HOW TO USE THIS BOOK

There are two ways to use this book:

1. There's a straightforward index at the back. If you know somewhere already (and it's any good) you should find it here. Numbers refer to page numbers.

2. The book can be used by categories, e.g. you can look up the best French restaurants or the best pubs with outdoor drinking. Each entry has an item number in the outside margin. These are in numerical order and allow easy cross-referencing.

   The categories are further divided up into groups, e.g. Where to Stay, Where to Eat. Each group has a map, on which are pinpointed the most important locations within the whole group, e.g. The Best Hotels. The maps cover the city centre only and are not to scale. They are intended to be diagrammatic only. Each entry has a map reference which can be found beneath the item number in the border. If an item is out of the centre, an arrow indicates its direction off the map. In the border this is denoted by an x, e.g. xD4 means 'Off the map at square D4'.

TICKS FOR THE BEST THERE IS

Although everything listed in the book is notable and remarkable in some way, there are places that are outstanding even in this superlative company. Instead of marking them with a rosette or a star, they have been 'awarded' a tick, the symbol of the … *the Best!* guides.

 Among the very best in Scotland

 Among the best (of its type) in the UK

 Among the best (of its type) in the world, or simply unique

A NOTE ON CATEGORIES

The book is arranged in five categories: Where to Stay; Where to Eat; Where to Drink; Where to Go (for general activities) in Town; and Where to Go out of Town. Within these five sections, categories range from the (mainly) very expensive, e.g. Best Hotels, to the fairly cheap, e.g. Best Hostels. The final section, Where to go out of Town, lists places near to the city, easily reached by car or public transport and for a range of interests. Like most of the other items in *Edinburgh the Best!*, these have been extracted from *Scotland the Best!*, which covers the whole of the country.

THE CODES

1. The Item Code

At the outside margin of every item is a code which will enable you to find it on a map. Thus **152** *D3* should be read as follows: **152** is the item number, listed in a simple consecutive order; *D3* is the map coordinate, to help pinpoint the item's location on the map grid. A coordinate such as *xE1* indicates that the item can be reached by leaving the map at grid reference *E1*.

2. The Hotel Codes

Below each hotel recommended is a band of codes as follows:

20RMS   JAN-DEC   T/T   PETS   CC   KIDS   TOS   LOTS

20RMS means the hotel has 20 bedrooms in total. No differentiation is made as to the type of room. Most hotels will offer twin rooms as singles or put extra beds in doubles if required. This code merely gives an impression of size.

JAN-DEC means the hotel is open all year round. APR-OCT means approximately from the beginning of April to the end of October.

T/T refers to the facilities: T/ means there are direct-dial phones in the bedrooms, while /T means there are TVs in the bedrooms.

PETS means the hotel accepts dogs and other pets, probably under certain conditions (e.g. pets should be kept in the bedroom). It's usually best to check first.

XPETS indicates that the hotel does not generally accept pets.

CC means the hotel accepts major credit cards (e.g. Access, Visa).

XCC means the hotel does not accept major credit cards.

KIDS indicates children are welcome and special provisions/rates may be available.

XKIDS does not necessarily mean that children are not able to accompany their parents, only that special provisions/rates are not usually made. Check by phone.

TOS means the hotel is part of the Taste of Scotland scheme and has been selected for having a menu which features imaginative cooking using Scottish ingredients. The Taste of Scotland produces an annual guide of members.

LOTS Rooms which cost more than £60 per night per person. The theory is that if you can afford over £120 a room, it doesn't matter too much if it's £125 or £150. Other price bands are:

EXP Expensive: £50-60 per person.

MED.EXP Medium (expensive): £38-50.

MED.INX Medium (inexpensive): £28-38.

INX Inexpensive: £20-28.

CHP Cheap: less than £20.

Rates are per person per night. They are worked out by halving the published average rate for a twin room in high season and should be used only to give an impression of cost. They are based on 1997 prices. Add between £2 and £5 per year, though the band should stay the same unless the hotel undergoes improvements.

3. The Restaurant Code

Found at the bottom right of all restaurant entries. It refers to the price of an average dinner per person with a starter, a main course and a dessert. It doesn't include wine, coffee or extras.

EXP Expensive: more than £30.

MED Medium: £20-30.

INX Inexpensive: £12-20.

CHP Cheap: less than £12.

These are based on 1997 rates. With inflation, the relative price bands should stay about the same.

4. The Walk Codes

A number of walks are described in the book. Below each walk is a band of codes as follows:

2-10km   CIRC   BIKE   1-A-1

2-10km means the walk(s) described may vary in length from 2km to 10km.

CIRC means the walk can be circular, while **XCIRC** shows the walk is not circular and you must return more or less by the way you came.

BIKE indicates the walk has a path which is suitable for ordinary bikes.

XBIKE means the walk is not suitable for, or does not permit, cycling.

MTBIKE means the track is suitable for mountain or all-terrain bikes.

The **1-A-1** Code

First number (**1, 2, 3**) indicates how easy the walk is.

1 the walk is easy; **2** medium difficulty, e.g. standard hillwalking, not dangerous nor requiring special knowledge or equipment; **3** difficult: care, preparation and a map are needed.

The letters (**A, B, C**) indicate how easy it is to find the path.

A the route is easy to find. The way is either marked or otherwise obvious; **B** the route is not very obvious, but you'll get there; **C** you will need a map and preparation or a guide.

The last number (**1, 2, 3**) indicates what to wear on your feet.

1 ordinary outdoor shoes, including trainers, are probably OK unless the ground is very wet; **2** you will need walking boots; **3** you will need serious walking or hiking boots.

Apart from the designated walks, the **1-A-1** code is employed wherever there is more than a short stroll required to get somewhere, e.g. a waterfall or a monument. The code appears at the bottom-right corner of the item.

LIST OF ABBREVIATIONS

As well as codes and because of obvious space limitations, a personal short-hand and ad hoc abbreviation system has had to be created. I'm the first to admit some may be annoying, especially 'restau' for restaurant, but it's a long word and it comes up often. The others which are used are:

accom	accommodation	incl	including
adj	adjacent	inexp	inexpensive
admn	admission	info	information
app	approach	jnct	junction
approx	approximately	L	loch
atmos	atmosphere	LO	last orders
av	average	min(s)	minute(s)
ave	avenue	N	north
AYR	all year round	no smk	no smoking
bedrms	bedrooms	nr	near
betw	between	NTS	National Trust for Scotland
br	bridge		
BYOB	bring your own bottle	o/look(s)	overlook(s)/ing
cl	closes/closed	opp	opposite
cres	crescent	o/side	outside
dining-rm	dining-room	pl	place
dr	drive	poss	possible
E	east	pt	point/port
Edin	Edinburgh	R	river
esp	especially	r/bout	roundabout
excl	excluding	rd	road
exhib(s)	exhibition(s)	refurb	refurbished/ment
exp	expensive	restau	restaurant
facs	facilities	rm(s)	room(s)
ft	fort	rt	right
Glas	Glasgow	S	south
gr	great	sq	square
grd(s)	garden(s)	st	street
hr(s)	hour(s)	stn	station
HS	Historic Scotland	SYHA	Scottish Youth Hostels Association

terr	terrace	v	very
TO	tourist information office	vac	vacation
		vegn	vegetarian
t/off	turn-off	W	west
trad	traditional	w/end(s)	weekend(s)
tratt	trattoria	yr(s)	year(s)
univ	university		

WHERE TO STAY

THE MALMAISON 'award-winning, praise-laden designer hotel' (page 18)

THE BEST HOTELS

1
D2
✔ ✔ **THE BALMORAL:** 556 2414. Princes St at E end above Waverley Stn. Capital landmark with its clock always 2 min fast (except at Hogmanay) so you don't miss your train. The old pile especially dear to Sir Rocco Forte's heart. Exp for a mere tourist but if you can't afford to stay there's always afternoon tea in the Palm Court. Few hotels anywhere are so much in the heart of things. Good business centre, fine sports facs; luxurious and distinctive rms with some ethereal views of the city. Main restau, Number One Princes Street (75/BEST RESTAUS), excellent, and less formal brasserie, Hadrian's, adequate.

186RMS JAN-DEC T/T PETS CC KIDS LOTS

2
C3
✔ ✔ **THE CALEDONIAN:** 459 9988. Princes St, W End. Edin institution – former stn hotel built in 1903. Owners have spent a fortune upgrading it from merely grand to Grand and Businesslike, and at the time of writing is up for sale so new ownership likely. Sparkling spa (with pool). Endearing lack of uniformity about the rms. Executive rms on fifth floor (and deluxe rms elsewhere) have gr views as well as facs. Main restau, The Pompadour, also refurb for fine dining, Chisholm's brasserie is a ... brasserie. Cally Bar a famous rendezvous.

249RMS JAN-DEC T/T XPETS CC KIDS TOS LOTS

3
xE4
✔ ✔ **PRESTONFIELD HOUSE:** 668 3346. Off Priestfield Rd, 3km S of city centre. The Heilan' coos in the 14-acre grounds tell you this isn't your average urban bed for the night. 17th-century building with period features still intact. Architect Sir William Adam, responsible for the ceiling in the Tapestry Rm, also 'did' the ornamental ceilings in Holyroodhouse. Bulk of rms more recent (1997) and older have more character. Restau gets mixed reviews.

31RMS JAN-DEC T/T PETS CC XKIDS LOTS

4
B2
✔ **CHANNINGS:** 315 2226. S Learmonth Grds, parallel to Queensferry Rd after Dean Br. Tasteful alternative to hotel chain hospitality. 5 period town houses joined to form a v tasteful and discreet hotel. Impeccable décor with efficient and individual service. Gr views from top-floor rms, incl the Prime Minister's alma mater – Fettes College. A chic retreat from downtown throngs. Brasserie has 2 AA rosettes.

48RMS JAN-DEC T/T XPETS CC KIDS LOTS

5
C1
✔ **THE HOWARD:** 557 3500. 36 Gr King St. Elegant establishment in the heart of the New Town – gr individual rms with cupboards big enough for a horse and some baths ditto. Basement restau, Number 36, is one of the

city's finest (72/BEST RESTAUS) and a marked design contrast to what's upstairs. Same owners as Channings (*see above*).

15RMS JAN-DEC T/T XPETS CC XKIDS TOS LOTS

6   **ROYAL TERRACE:** 557 3222. 18 Royal Terr. Romanesque plunge pool,
E2   other sports facs, multi-level terraced grd out back, deceptively large number of rms and town house décor a tad on the Baroque side. In other words, fabulous darling! Bar/restau not so notable among the natives, so good place for discreet meets.

110RMS JAN-DEC T/T XPETS CC KIDS LOTS

7   **HOLIDAY INN CROWN PLAZA:** 557 9797. 80 High St. Modern but sym-
D3   pathetic building on the Royal Mile, handy for everything. Good facs but some say service lacking. Thin walls, not gr views. Piano bar can be fun if taken in the right spirit (lots of). Gym and small pool. Unlike other hotels nr here, does have parking.

238RMS JAN-DEC T/T PETS CC KIDS TOS LOTS

8   **THE SHERATON:** 229 9131. Festival Sq on Lothian Rd and nr Conference
C3   Centre, this city-centre business hotel won no prizes for architecture when it opened late 1980s, but it's settling in now and the 'square' is look-ing better. A reliable stopover with excellent service. Larger rms and cas-tle views carry premiums, but make big difference. Terr restau adequate, but The Grill menu prepared under the supervision of Nicolas Laurent is elegant, Scottish and innovative (3 Michelin Forks).

261RMS JAN-DEC T/T PETS CC KIDS TOS LOTS

9   **THE GEORGE:** 225 1251. George St (betw Hanover St and St Andrew Sq).
C2   An Inter-Continental Hotel but dating back to late 18th century. Good views to Fife from the top 2 floors. Pricey, but you pay for the location and the Georgian niceties. Busy and grandiose carvery plus good Gallic restau, the Chambertin (103/FRENCH RESTAUS). Good Hogmanay hotel if you like a touch of carnival – the Latin stage is outside. Taken over by luvvies during TV Festival.   **195RMS JAN-DEC T/T PETS CC KIDS LOTS**

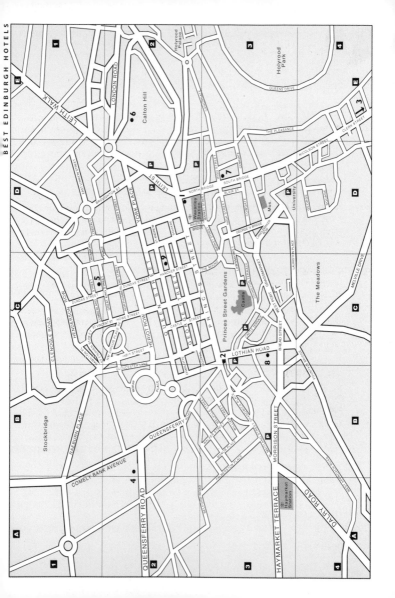

THE MORE INDIVIDUAL HOTELS (AND GUEST HOUSES)

10
xE1

✓✓ **THE MALMAISON:** 468 5000. Tower Pl, Leith, at the dock gates. Award-winning, praise-laden designer hotel with individual and rather natty rms. Appeals to smart, young thrusting types like me and Robbie Williams. CD players in each *chambre* (borrow CDs from reception). Brasserie and café-bar have stylish ambience too (91/BEST BISTROS) and there are many others nearby in this waterfront quarter. Also in Glas, Newcastle, Manchester and spreading.

60RMS JAN-DEC T/T PETS CC KIDS EXP

11
C3

✓✓ **THE POINT:** 221 5555. 34 Bread St. You'd never guess this used to be a Co-operative department store. Space and colour combinations manage to look simultaneously rich and minimal, some castle views. Suites (LOTS) come with side-lit Jacuzzis. Considered one of the gr designery hotels in world terms and features on the cover of *Hotel Design*. Café-bar Monboddo and restau have modern and spacious, mid-Euro feel. Good places to meet Edinburgers.

140RMS JAN-DEC T/T PETS CC KIDS EXP

12
B3

✓✓ **THE BONHAM:** 226 6050. 35 Drumsheugh Grds. Discreet town-house in elegant W End cres. Cosmo service and ambience. *Conde Naste Travel* called it 'one of the coolest' (in the world). Owned by same people as the Howard and Channings (4/5/BEST HOTELS). Rms stylish but not minimalist. Dining in calm, spacious restau where chef Pelham Hill excels. No bar. **48RMS JAN-DEC T/T XPETS CC XKIDS LOTS**

13
C3

✓ **INNER SANCTUM** and the **OLD RECTORY** at the **WITCHERY:** 225 5613. Castlehill. 2 highly individual rms and an apartment above the Witchery restau (71/BEST RESTAUS) at the top of the Royal Mile. Prob the most exceptional and atmospheric in town – designed by owner James Thomson and Mark Rowley – fairly camp/theatrical, OTT and v sexy. Go with somebody good. **2+1 APT JAN-DEC T/T XPETS CC XKIDS LOTS**

14
B3

✓ **EDINBURGH RESIDENCE:** 226 3380. 7 Rothesay Terr. Another town house affair, this where several Georgian town houses have been joined into an elegant *residencia* (or time-share). Usually rms (or suites available), but pricey. No restau but 24 hr room service. Drawing rm if you're feeling lonely. Quiet W End but nr nightlife and shops.

21RMS (8 SUITES) JAN-DEC T/T XPETS CC KIDS LOTS

15   **SIBBET HOUSE, 26 NORTHUMBERLAND ST:** 556 1078. The definitive
C2   New Town B & B. Some rms adj and apartment over the way. Georgian
town house hospitality that has been wowing guests for yrs. Timeless.
8RMS(+APT) JAN-DEC T/T XPETS CC KIDS MED.EXP

16   **24 NORTHUMBERLAND ST:** 556 8140. Next door to 26 above, so simi-
C2   lar apartments – these full of antiques (owner is notable dealer). Several
people wrote to suggest this place for inclusion. It's been a secret so far –
now you'll have to book.   **3RMS JAN-DEC X/X XPETS CC XKIDS MED.EXP**

17   **17 ABERCROMBY PLACE:** 557 8036. Another plush and private
C2   Georgian town house; discreet lack of signage. Once abode of the New
Town's architect, Playfair, now belongs to advocate Eirlys Lloyd. No smk, 2
rms in a self-contained mews; main house for breakfast.
8RMS JAN-DEC T/T XPETS CC KIDS MED.EXP

18   **THE ALBANY:** 556 0397. 39 Albany St. Refurb town-house hotel handy
D2   for trend-spotting Broughton St, but too exp for its denizens. New Town
splendour and *politesse* – only a few mins walk uphill to Princes St.
Basement restau, Haldane's (150/SCOTTISH RESTAUS), is pretty good.
21RMS JAN-DEC T/T PETS CC KIDS LOTS

19   **THE GRANGE:** 667 5681. 8 Whitehouse Terr. In southern sedate suburb
xD4   and set in beautiful grds, this is a quiet country-house kind of retreat from
which to venture into the city (centre 3km). Restau but we haven't tried.
15RMS JAN-DEC T/T PETS CC KIDS EXP

20   **SIX ST MARY'S PLACE:** 332 8965. Vegn GH. On main st of Stockbridge
B1   (St Mary's Pl part of Raeburn Pl) and busy main rd out of town for Forth
Rd Br and N, this is a tastefully converted Georgian town house. Informal,
friendly, well-cared-for accom popular with academics and people we
like. No smk. Vegn breakfast in conservatory. Jolly; nice people.
8RMS JAN-DEC X/X XPETS CC KIDS MED.INX

21   **STUART HOUSE:** 557 9030. 12 E Claremont St. Nr the corner of main rd
D1   and pleasant walk up to Princes St (1.5km). Residential New Town st and
family house decorated with taste and attention to detail – bonny flower
grd out front. Book well in advance. No smk.
5RMS JAN-DEC T/T XPETS CC KIDS MED.EXP

22   **TEVIOTDALE HOUSE:** 667 4376. 53 Grange Loan, towards E End.
xD4   Fabulous fecund flower grd out front and bargain accom within. Ground-
floor rm (popular with honeymooners) has a 4-poster with adj chaise

longue and the whole effect is undeniably, unexpectedly sexy – although v respectable you understand. Healthy breakfasts.

7RMS JAN-DEC T/T XPETS CC KIDS MED.INX

23
xE1

HOTEL JAVA: 467 7527. Constitution St, Leith, next to the estimable Port O' Leith (257/GR EDIN PUBS). Friendly, contemporary bar with basic but inexp rms in Leith nr docks and with many of the city's best bars and restaus nearby. Phillipa and Sue run a laid-back and happy house. Rms at back and round courtyard. **10RMS JAN-DEC X/X PETS CC KIDS CHP**

24
D3

TAYLORS HALL: 622 6800. Cowgate. If you don't mind the racket (or want to be part of it), this is a clubby/young thing kind of hotel in the heart of the throbbing Cowgate area and above the hugely popular Three Sisters pub (269/GR EDIN PUBS). 3 bars to choose from (Irish/American/Goth), 24 hr license for residents. Can do 4 in a rm.

42RMS JAN-DEC T/T PETS CC XKIDS MED.EXP

25
C2

FREDERICK HOUSE: 226 1999. 42 Frederick St nr George St. Central refurb making the most of its location and booming Edin to charge a tad over the odds for basic though contemp facs. Breakfast over the rd at Café Rouge for example. **42RMS JAN-DEC T/T XPETS CC XKIDS MED.EXP**

26
B3

WEST END HOTEL: 225 3656. 35 Palmerston Pl. Capital haunt for Highlanders and Islanders who feel like a blether in Gaelic or a good folk music session in the bar (decent measures). Popular with folkie non-guests too. Spacious rms with oddly familiar furniture.

8RMS JAN-DEC T/T XPETS CC KIDS INX

27
E2

PARLIAMENT HOUSE: 478 4000. 15 Calton Hill. Good central location, only 200m from E end of Princes St and adj to Calton Hill (369/BEST VIEWS), although tucked away. Small bar in residents lounge and recent ('99) restau for breakfast, evening meals – but OK town house-style décor.

53RMS JAN-DEC T/T XPETS CC KIDS EXP

28
D3

STATION HOTEL: 226 1446. 9-13 Market St, behind Waverley Stn. Some good views from upper floors to Princes St. Couldn't be handier for the stn or city centre. Rms feel a bit 'holiday package deal', basic but acceptable. No smk. Its restau is Italian-ish and curiously, always empty.

30RMS JAN-DEC T/T XPETS CC KIDS MED.EXP

THE BEST 'ECONOMY' HOTELS AND TRAVEL-LODGES

Hotels/B&Bs below are included on grounds of price, convenience or just because we like them for some idiosyncratic reason.

29
C3
APEX INTERNATIONAL: 300 3456. 31-35 Grassmarket. Once part of Heriot-Watt Univ, a determined conversion resulted in a central hotel with contemporary Euro-bland facade. Civilized although a tad characterless and no longer inx. Rms with castle view are more exp, but worth the extra. Fifth-floor restau (INX) also has nice outlook. Another Apex (474 3456) nr Haymarket with 68 rms and a restau called Tabu (mixed reviews).
168RMS JAN-DEC T/T XPETS CC KIDS EXP

30
xA3
STAKIS EDINBURGH AIRPORT: 519 4400. At the airport, 10km W of city centre. No way 'economy', but a reliable travellers' tryst. An L-shaped box with the buzz of a high-class transit camp; charming staff. You can virtually roll out of bed and check in. That smell over the airport by the way is due to some unconscionable thing they do to chickens in their concentration camp nearby. Stay indoors and don't have the fricassee!
134RMS JAN-DEC T/T XPETS CC KIDS LOTS

31
B3
TRAVEL INN: 228 9819. 1 Morrison Link, nr Haymarket Stn. Likeable for the fact it makes no pretence to be anything other than a bed factory. Big, orthogonal and dull but v cheap – flat charge of under £40 applies per rm which can take 2 adults or a family of 4. 7 rms specially adapted for wheelchair users.
280RMS JAN-DEC X/T XPETS CC KIDS CHP

32
xA3
FORTE POSTHOUSE: 334 0390. Corstorphine Rd next to Zoo. Entrance feels like an underground car park, but there's a gr view across to the Pentlands. Bit of a featureless bed box, although recently refurbed, but has all the facs expected of a bed box hotel. You hear real wolves howling in the night.
303RMS JAN-DEC T/T PETS CC KIDS MED.EXP

33
C3
PREMIER LODGE: 220 2299. 94-96 Grassmarket. Basic and boisterously located accom next to Biddy Mulligan's which is open to 1am, but hotel now soundproofed. Still, o/side the Grassmarket is fairly full-on, so good for party animal business types on a budget. Don't bring grandma, do come on a night out with the lads (or lassies).
44RMS JAN-DEC X/T PETS CC KIDS MED.INX

34
D3
IBIS: 240 7000. Hunter Sq. First in Scotland of the Euro budget chain and first in Edin of a huge rash of Parliament boom hotels. Dead central

behind the Tron so good for Hogmanay stays (or not). Serviceable and efficient. For tourists, poss the best of the ones above for location.

99RMS JAN-DEC T/T PETS CC KIDS MED.INX

35
E3
TRAVEL LODGE: 557 6281 (or central booking 0800 850950). 33 St Mary's St. Edin central version of national (often roadside) chain. All usual, formulaic facs but inx and nr Royal Mile (Holyrood end) and Cowgate for late-night action. Basic bar/café for breakfast and rendezvous.

193RMS JAN-DEC T/T XPETS CC KIDS INX

THE BEST HOSTELS

Edin has some YHA hostels (nae drinking) and independents (young and Hoochy, open 24 hrs), also some handy univ halls of residence to let o/side term time. With all the independent hostels, it's best to turn up around 11/11.30am if you haven't booked. The SYHA is the Scottish Youth Hostels Association, 01786 891400.

36
D3
✓ ✓ **ROYAL MILE BACKPACKERS (THE HIGH STREET HOSTEL):** 557 6120. 105 High St. On the Royal Mile, nr the Cowgate with its late-night bars. Ideal central cheap 24 hr crash-out dormitory accom with all the facs for itinerant youth seeking a capital experience. At the time of writing, the original hostel also called **THE HIGH ST HOSTEL** (557 3984), but at 8 Blackfriars St and under threat from the neighbouring Holiday Inn, was still open. Original here means best. Sister hostel: **CASTLE ROCK**, 15 Johnston Terr (225 9666) in the old Council Environmental Health HQ, is huge (190 beds in various dorms, but no singles/doubles) and has some gr views across the Grassmarket or to the castle which is just over there. Same folk (Mr Backpacker himself, Peter Macmillan) also have places in Ft William, Inverness, Oban and Skye.
CHP

37
A3
✓ ✓ **S.Y. HOSTEL, EGLINTON:** 337 1120. 18 Eglinton Cres. From the stained glass over the main door to the tartan and wood entrance foyer, you know you're not in a typical hostel. Grand late-Victorian pile in a quiet W End st with 156 beds – majority in dorms but some rms for 4 (single sex dorms). Members only but you can join at reception. Booking recommended. Doors locked at 2am.
CHP

38
A2
✓ **BELFORD HOSTEL:** 225 6209. Douglas Grds, nr Gallery of Modern Art (excellent café, 199/BEST TEAROOMS) and quaint Dean Village, but

still fairly central. Bizarre concept – 98 beds in partitioned-off 'rms' of 6-10 in a converted church. Top-bunk berth gets you a view of the vaulted wooden ceiling way above. Games rm, bar, MTV. Sister establishment **EDINBURGH BACKPACKERS HOSTEL**, 65 Cockburn St (220 1717), is closer to action. **CHP**

39
D2 **PRINCES ST HOSTEL:** 556 6894. 5 W Register St. Behind Burger King at E end of Princes St. Incredibly central for cheap accom. Basic and attracts the usual international crowd. Same people now have **PRINCES ST WEST**, 3 Queensferry St (226 2939) with bar. **CHP**

40
xC4 **S.Y. HOSTEL, BRUNTSFIELD:** 447 2994. 7 Bruntsfield Cres. S of Tollcross about 10 min walk from W End. Buses from Princes St (grd side), nos 11, 15, 16. Reliable and secure hostel accom in a verdant corner of Bruntsfield. 130 beds but booking 2-3 months in advance is essential at peak times. Again, members only, join at reception and doors locked at 2am. **CHP**

41
D3 From July-Sep, SYHA also opens a temporary hostel in **ROBERTSON'S CLOSE** off Cowgate. Phone Edin district office for info 229 8660.

42
xE4 **POLLOCK HALLS:** 667 0662. Off Dalkeith Rd. The main accom for Edin Univ – a village of modern low-rise blocks, situated 3km S of centre next to the Royal Commonwealth Swimming Pool (354/MAIN ATTRACTIONS) and in the shadow of Arthur's Seat (366/BEST WALKS), on which to gaze or jog. Refectory, bar, shared kitchens and showers. Huge number of rms – 800 basic singles and more than 400 others, some doubles. Vacs only. **MED.INX**

43
xC4 **NAPIER UNIVERSITY:** 455 4621. Craiglockhart campus off Colinton Rd. College halls in high-rise blocks about 10km SW of centre. In grounds of imposing Craiglockhart Hospital where Siegfried Sassoon met Wilfred Owen. Far out for some, but good sports facs, incl pool. Vacs only. **CHP**

44
xA2 **QUEEN MARGARET COLLEGE:** 317 3310. Clerwood Terr. Way out, midway betw main rds W to Glas and N to Forth Br; about 10km, so transport probably essential (or bus). Campus facs, e.g. refectory, laundry, bank, good sports. Shared bathrms, etc. and a bit dreary, so not exceptional value, but a private and well-equipped refuge from uptown hassles. Phone first. Also self-catering flats. Vacs only. **CHP**

45
xD4 **ARGYLE PLACE:** 667 9991. 14 Argyle Pl, in Marchmont area of up-market student flats. Quiet area though Argyle Pl the most happening st. 2 km to centre across 'The Meadows' (not advised for women at night). Nice grd. **CHP**

THE BEST CAMPING AND CARAVAN PARKS

Refer to Lothians map on pages 116–117.

46
D1

✔ **THE MONKS' MUIR:** 01620 860340. 4km S of Haddington and sign-posted off A1 40km from centre. Convenient location (good rd to town) and attractive site. Good shop and bike hire point. Floodlit *terrain de pétanque* (here they do try harder). 67 pitches. Open AYR.

47
C2

MORTONHALL PARK: 664 1533. Off Frogston Rd E, a kind of inner-city ring rd. About 12km S of centre. From S and city bypass: take Lothianburn jnct into town and rt at first lights for 4km. From centre: take A702 via Morningside to last left turn before bypass. Mortonhall marked, but enter via (and pass) Klondyke Grd Centre. No. 7 or 11 bus from town. Well-equipped park with 4 toilet/shower blocks, shop, laundry, lounge, play area and fully serviced pitches. Also bar/restau in converted stables/courtyard serving food till 9pm. Coffee shop with decent home-baking at grd centre. Mar-Oct. 268 places.

48
C1

THE EDINBURGH CARAVAN CLUB SITE: 312 6874. Marine Dr, Silverknowes. 8km NW of centre via Ferry Rd then rt on Pennywell Rd, continue over r/bout to Marine Dr. Former local authority site, taken over and substantially refurbed by the Caravan Club of GB – reopened 1997. Accepts non-members. 150 pitches for caravans, tents and motor homes – all with electricity. Two heated toilet blocks, laundry, disabled facs. Open AYR.

49
C2

FORDEL, DALKEITH: 660 3921. Lauder Rd. On A68, 4km S of Dalkeith; 18km SE of centre. V well equipped and serviced site secluded from the busy rd. Behind a 24 hr garage and pub/café (Fordel Inn). Some work done recently so improved pitches and more landscaping. Best to have a car; reasonable bus service to Dalkeith, but fewer go past gate. 35 caravan sites, 100 pitches.

50
C1

DRUM MOHR, MUSSELBURGH: 665 6867. Levenhall. 4km out of Musselburgh on the coast rd to Prestonpans. 22km E of centre. Go through Musselburgh, signed off bypass and take rd rt at Mining Museum. Award-winning site is 400m up a country lane, within sight of the sea, quiet (apart from some traffic noise) and well maintained. You will be rather removed from Edin, but within easy reach of the golf/beach-es/walks and ice cream of E Lothian. Disabled facs. Mar-Oct. 120 pitches.

THE BEST HOTELS OUTSIDE TOWN

Refer to Lothians map on pages 116–117.

51
D1 ✓ ✓ **GREYWALLS, GULLANE:** 01620 842144. On the coast, 36km E of Edin off A198 just beyond golfers' paradise of Gullane. O/looks Muirfield, the championship course (no right of access) and nr Gullane's 3 courses and N Berwick's 2 (384/385/SPORTS FACS). No grey walls here but warm sandstone and light, summery public rms in this Lutyens-designed manor with grds attributed to Gertrude Jekyll. It's the look that makes it special and the roses are legendary. Sculpture grd in July and literary w/ends. Library like a London club, and service. Golf ain't everything.
23RMS APR-OCT T/T PETS CC XKIDS TOS LOTS

52
B1 ✓ ✓ **CHAMPANY INN:** 01506 834532. On A904, 3km from Linlithgow on way to Forth Rd Bridge and S Queensferry. Exemplary restau with rms format with 16 comfortable rms annexed to the restau which is legendary for steaks and seafood (183/BURGERS AND STEAKS). Lovely rm for breakfast. Extraordinary wine-list with dinner. Veggies should not venture here.
16RMS JAN-DEC T/T XPETS CC KIDS LOTS

53
C2 ✓ **BORTHWICK CASTLE, NORTH MIDDLETON:** 01875 820514. On B6367, 3km off the A7, 18km bypass, 26km SE of centre. So this is a real Border castle, a big red one. Walls 30m high, this magnificent tower house knocks you off your horse with its authenticity – Mary Queen of Scots was blockaded here once and at night you expect to see her swishing up the spiral stairs. 8 rms in castle, 2 in gatehouse, the (v) grand banqueting hall is impressive, dinner (EXP) is not.
10RMS MAR-DEC T/X PETS CC KIDS LOTS

54
B1 ✓ **NORTON HOUSE, INGLISTON:** 333 1275. Off A8 nr airport, 10km W of city centre. Virgin hotel in extensive grounds (hence quiet) with those Bransonesque touches you'll love or loathe – teddy bear on the bed, ducks in the bath. But high standard of service and accom with country house feel and handy for airport, points N or SW, even Edin. Conservatory restau is easily worth its two AA rosettes.
47RMS JAN-DEC T/T XPETS CC KIDS TOS LOTS

55
C2 **JOHNSTOUNBURN HOUSE, HUMBIE:** 01875 833696. On B6457 2km from A68 and 25km SE of centre. Bypass 22km. Country class in this 17th-century manor with relaxed and friendly service. Some rms in its coach

house, all have that upbeat frilliness. Public areas v cool, esp the panelled 18th-century dining-rm. Feels like a true escape. Dinner so-so, good wine-list.

20RMS JAN-DEC T/T PETS CC KIDS TOS LOTS

56 **DALHOUSIE CASTLE, BONNYRIGG:** 01875 820153. Just off B704 2km
C2 from the A7, 15km from bypass and 23km S of centre. The castle that tries too hard? It looks fantastic in its setting and dates way back to the 13th century but the facs are everything you would expect from a contemporary city hotel, which is perversely disappointing. (Previous guests incl Edward I, Cromwell, Queen Victoria, some rock stars.) Our Braveheart researcher was quite fond of the William Wallace rm; dinner is taken in the dungeon. Another 5 rms in adj Victorian lodge.

34RMS JAN-DEC T/T PETS CC KIDS TOS LOTS

57 **HOUSTON HOUSE, UPHALL:** 01506 853831. On A899 at end of
B1 Broxburn/Uphall Main St, 8km from r/bout at the start of the M8 Edin–Glas motorway. Airport 10km, 18km W of centre. Bits of this tower house date to the 16th century, others far more recent (extension with 46 rms). Yet more 4-posters, nice open fire in the bar, restau is rated and the place is stuffed with farmers during Royal Highland Show week. Set on 20 acres of greenery, atypical Uphall. Sports facs, incl a pool.

71RMS JAN-DEC T/T XPETS CC KIDS TOS LOTS

58 **DALMAHOY, KIRKNEWTON:** 333 1845. On A71 (Kilmarnock rd) on
B2 edge of town – bypass 5km, 15km W of centre, airport 6km. In the beginning was the word, and the word was golf. 2 good courses, European Tour venue and that's what the groups of chaps (and occasionally ladies) come for. Hotel itself is Georgian with 7 distinctive rms, rest in new annex where the extensive sports facs reside. Part of the Marriott chain. 60 new rms '99.

215RMS JAN-DEC T/T XPETS CC KIDS TOS LOTS

59 **MARINE HOTEL, NORTH BERWICK:** 01620 892406. The grand old sea-
D1 side hotel of N Berwick reeks of holidays gone by – you almost expect to see Margaret Rutherford on the putting green. Snooker, open-air swimming pool. O/looks links and Fidra. Good for kids and golf.

83RMS JAN-DEC T/T PETS CC KIDS EXP

60 **OPEN ARMS, DIRLETON:** 01620 850241. Dirleton is 4km from Gullane
D1 towards N Berwick. Comfortable if pricey hotel in centre of village, opp ruins of 13th-century castle. Location means it's a golfers' paradise and special packages are available. Restau has 2 AA whatsits.

10RMS JAN-DEC T/T PETS CC KIDS TOS LOTS

61 **HAWES INN, SOUTH QUEENSFERRY:** 331 1990. From city take rd N via
B1 Queensferry Rd heading for Forth Rd Br. On front at Hawes Pier and liter-
ally under the famous rail br (356/MAIN ATTRACTIONS). Pick the rt rm and lie
back in the 4-poster to soak up an atmos that made RLS escape into
Kidnapped. Facs far from fab, but genuine 16th century with unique situ-
ation. Some nights, many bikers.

8RMS (NONE EN SUITE) JAN-DEC T/T PETS CC KIDS MED.INX

62 **QUEENSFERRY LODGE HOTEL, nr NORTH QUEENSFERRY:** 01383
B1 410000. At Fife end of rd br (so Edin is a toll away), but a good stopping-
off place for all points N. Dramatic setting with estuarine views.
Restaus/bars/shop – a modern purpose-built roadhouse. N Queensferry
less crowded than S (except for Deep Sea World – 466/WHERE TO TAKE
KIDS); nice bistro – the Channel (01383 412567).

77RMS JAN-DEC T/T PETS CC KIDS MED.INX

63 **THE OLD ABERLADY INN:** 01875 870503. Main St. Straightforward drop
D1 inn with simple, well-kept rms, a good farmhouse-style bistro with inter-
esting menu and a trad howf for drinks and bar food. Popular with golfers
– OK for anyone. **8RMS JAN-DEC T/T PETS CC KIDS MED.INX**

64 **TWEEDDALE ARMS, GIFFORD:** 01620 810240. One of 2 inns in this
D2 heart of E Lothian village 9km from the A1 at Haddington, within easy
reach of Edin. Set among rich farming country, Gifford is conservative and
couthy. Some bedrms small, but public rms pleasant if chintzy. Smells like
a country inn should. **16RMS JAN-DEC T/T PETS CC KIDS MED.INX**

THE POINT 'you'd never guess this used to be a Co-operative department store' (page 18)

WHERE TO EAT

Stockbridge

COMELY BANK AVENUE
QUEENSFERRY ROAD
RAEBURN PLACE
GLENOGLE ROAD
HENDERSON ROW
INDIA STREET
GLOUCESTER LANE
HERIOT ROW
HOWE STREET
ST VINCENT ST
DUNDAS STREET
GREAT KING STREET
GEORGE STREET
PRINCES STREET
ROSE STREET
HANOVER STREET
CASTLE STREET
FREDERICK STREET
QUEEN STREET

LEITH WALK
LONDON ROAD
Calton Hill
Holyrood Palace
Holyrood Park
QUEENS DRIVE
THE PLEASANCE
CLERK STREET
NICOLSON STREET
University
Mus.
GEORGE IV BRIDGE
SOUTH BRIDGE
NORTH BRIDGE
BLAIR ST
Waverley Station
WAVERLEY BRIDGE
Princes Street Gardens
Castle
LOTHIAN ROAD
WEST PORT
GRASSMARKET
BREAD STREET
LAURISTON PLACE
The Meadows
MELVILLE DRIVE

QUEENSFERRY STREET
MORRISON STREET
HAYMARKET TERRACE
Haymarket Station
DALRY ROAD

York Place
Leith St

68
74
78
73
66
75
72
69
70
67
71
65
70

A B C D E
1 2 3 4

THE BEST RESTAURANTS

65
C3
✓ ✓ **THE ATRIUM:** 228 8882. Foyer of the Traverse Theatre (410/NIGHTLIFE), Cambridge St off Lothian Rd. Can it really be 7 yrs since the Atrium opened and immediately became the top meal in town? Well it is, and it's remarkable how it has seen off newer and flashier rivals. Still simple and stylish with sharp service; the funkiest fine dining in the capital tonight. **BLUE** upstairs (79/BEST BISTROS) complements perfectly. Lunch Mon-Fri, dinner Mon-Sat. LO 10pm.   **EXP**

66
xE2
✓ ✓ **LA POTINIÈRE:** 01620 843214. Main St, Gullane. 36km W of city on A198 coast rd off A1. David and Hilary Brown's intimate, much-celebrated caff, the first truly gr restau in SE Scotland, enduring elegance although facing that stiff competition in town. I came back here summer of '99 after a long absence – it *is* still *the* best and worth the 45 min drive for the elegant simplicity of their set menu of French classic and contemporary cooking. Outstanding wine list. Dinner Fri-Sat only (or groups by arrangement). Lunch Tue-Sun. Famously booked in advance, but lunch and Fri easier and often cancellations. No smk.   **MED**

67
D3
✓ ✓ **THE TOWER:** 225 3003. Corner of Chambers St and George IV Br above the new Museum of Scotland. Top-end and top-floor restau in the distinctive 'tower' on the corner of the new museum building. Benefits from the much-admired grand design and detail of Gordon Benson's architectural vision. Décor has been described as retro-futurist; it feels that it could be anywhere except for Edin rooftops and castle skyline o/side the windows (and in summer, the terr). Gr private dining-rm in the tower itself. Kitchens far below in prehistoric Scotland, but food everything one would expect – Scottish slant on modern British. The steaks are good. 7 days. Lunch and dinner. LO 11pm. W/end booking essential. Smokers to the balcony!   **EXP**

68
xE1
✓ ✓ **(FITZ)HENRY:** 555 6625. 19 Shore Pl. Dave Ramsden's warehouse brasserie in an off-the-waterfront st in Leith – one of Edin's top spots and the only one (1997/98/99) apart from The Atrium (*see above*) to get a Michelin red M. Great chefs have come and gone – currently Brett Morman, a Sydney man. Fastidious, but non-intrusive service in a stylish setting. Lunch and dinner. Cl Sun.   **MED**

69
C2
✓ **RHODES & CO:** 220 9190. 3 Rose St opp M & S and Jenners, of which it is a part. Totally professional dining out experience from Gary, the Rhodes boy. High expectation so not always entirely realized. Stark, modern rm upstairs and bar by big windows on the street (with snackier

31

menu 11am-6pm, 7 days). Perhaps a bit soulless, but the Edin bourgeoisie
have taken to heart the fairly plain fare generally impeccably prepared
and presented without fuss (but not by Gary who has moved on). Mashed
potatoes, for example, and sticky toffee pud rarely come better than this.
Lunch 7 days. Dinner Mon-Sat. LO 10.30pm.   **MED**

70
xD4
✓ **THE MARQUE:** 466 6660. 19 Causewayside. Discreet Southside
bistro/restau owned by chefs Glyn Stevens and John Rutter. At first
('98) the 'menu you must', now settled into a more measured response.
Food v sound but smallish rm somewhat bereft of atmos. You feel you'd
bring your mum 'n' dad here on Graduation Day. They would be
impressed. Tue-Sun, lunch and dinner. LO 11pm.   **EXP**

71
C3
✓ **THE WITCHERY:** 225 5613. Castlehill. At the top of the Royal Mile
where the tourists come, many will be unaware that this is one of the
city's best restaus and certainly its most stylishly atmospheric. 2 salons,
the upper more witchery; in the 'secret grd' downstairs, a converted
school playground, James Thompson has created a more spacious ambience for the (same) elegant Scottish menu. 7 days. Lunch and dinner.
(235/LATE-NIGHT RESTAUS)   **EXP**

72
C1
✓ **NUMBER 36:** 556 3636. 36 Gr King St. Basement restau of the
Howard Hotel (5/BEST HOTELS) in the New Town and in design contrast to the Georgian opulence upstairs. Number 36 is bold and clean-cut
verging on minimalist. The food also is contemporary in every respect
and this is one of the city's great discreet eats. Innovative cuisine, service
is snappy. 7 days. Lunch and dinner (cl Sat lunch). No smk.   **MED**

73
xE1
✓ **MARTIN WISHART:** 553 3557. 54 The Shore. Small, chic restau on
the shore in Leith, formerly Silvios. Chef/prop the eponymous Martin
has trained with some big names to drop (but I won't). Some people rave
about this place (some don't). I'm on the fence, but can sometimes be
found in the window when I'm with the kind of friend who thinks that
food is the new rock 'n' roll. Contemp, stylish, no fuss – the food I mean!
Lunch Tue-Fri, dinner Tue-Sat.   **EXP**

74
xE1
✓ **THE VINTNER'S ROOM:** 554 6767. 87 Giles St, Leith. Cobbled courtyard to wine bar, with woody ambience and open fire. Vaults, formerly used to store claret (Leith was an important wine pt), also incl a
restau lit by candlelight. Bar and restau have same evening menu (French
tone using fresh Scottish produce), but cheaper options at lunch in the

bar and less formal. Excellent cheeseboard and wine list. Mon-Sat lunch and 6.30-10pm.   **MED**

75
D2 ✓ **NUMBER ONE PRINCES STREET, BALMORAL HOTEL:** 556 2414. Address with a certain ring for the principal restau of the Balmoral (1/BEST HOTELS) entered through lobby or off st. Based apparently on the Mandarin Grill, Hong Kong, these opulent subterranean salons have ample space around the tables, but the lighting and lacquering do little to cosify the ritziness. Chef Jeff Bland ensures that **HADRIAN'S BRASSERIE,** a peppermint lounge at st level, complements well. Cl Sat-Sun lunch. LO 10.30pm.   **EXP**

76
C2 ✓ **MARTIN'S:** 225 3106. 70 Rose St N Lane. Quiet lane behind busy shopping precinct nr Princes St – odd place to find a decent restau but this is one of Edin's most consistently top eateries. Good service, v high standard of contemporary cooking, delicate desserts and an unsurpassed, unpasteurized Celtic cheeseboard. Good on game and Martin knows his wines. 3 AA rosettes. Lunch Tue-Fri, dinner Tue-Sat. LO 10pm.   **EXP**

77
xE4 ✓ **BANKS:** 667 0707. 10 Newington Rd. Eponymous 2-tier restau of chef/proprietor Peter Banks who used to be at the Rock (*see below*). Eating out on the Southside moving up a notch here. À la carte upstairs excellent, and elegant dining and grill rm downstairs, mainly steaks and burgers (one fish, one veggie), is v good value. Real thick chips, exquisite desserts (both floors). Accolades imminent. Upstairs Tue-Sat (not Sat lunch). Grill 7 days, lunch and dinner. LO 10/10.30pm.   **INX.MED**

78
xE1 **THE ROCK:** 555 2225. Commercial St/Quay, Leith. In a row of 'waterfront' restaus in converted warehouses opp the new Scottish Office, this is the one that stands out for excellent food (though others are notable). Modern setup with good sightlines to other diners and open kitchen. Grill menu of burgers and steaks (and salmon) is simple and à la carte menu widens choice for non red-meaters. Mick Jagger and some women ate here '99. We hear changes may be afoot in 2000. 7 days. Lunch and dinner. Cl Sun lunch.   **MED**

THE BEST BISTROS AND CAFÉ-BARS

79
C3

✓✓ **BLUE:** 221 1222. Cambridge St. Upstairs in the Traverse Theatre building. From the makers of The Atrium (65/BEST RESTAUS), a lighter, informal lunch, indeed the same menu continues all day till late. Still one of most fashionable places in town to graze, you can eat for under a tenner; the menu, which changes seasonally, tempts you to more. Sound levels high, but partly because it's full of people with something to say. 12noon-3pm and 6-11pm daily. Set snacks only in the afternoon, bar open to 1am daily. It's where we go most easily. **CHP.INX**

80
xE1

✓✓ **SKIPPERS:** 554 1018. 1a Dock Pl. In a corner of Leith off Commercial Rd by the docks. Look for The Waterfront (*see opposite*) and bear left into adj cul-de-sac. The pioneer restau in the pre-yuppie Leith, it's still after all these yrs quite the best real bistro in town. V fishy, v quayside intimate and friendly. Look no further out to sea. Dinner Tue-Sat, LO 10pm. **MED**

81
C3

✓ **TUSCAN SQUARE:** 229 9859. 30 Grindlay St, part of the Lyceum Theatre (409/NIGHTLIFE). At last a formula in this site that has worked. Iain McMaster's light Mediterranean menu is of the moment, inx and v well done. Tables on the street for café-bar stuff. Upstairs for the evening (or 'suits' having lunch). Some big tables. Lunch and dinner. Cl Sun-Mon. **INX**

82
E4

✓ **HOWIE'S:** 668 2917. 75 St Leonard's St. Up on the Southside, this extended set of rms is always busy. Unfussy, extensive and eclectic menu the epitome of good Edin bistro food that's affordable. Totally reliable and inexp eating out. Though this is the original Howie's, 2 others hit the same spot S and W of the city. 63 Dalry Rd, 313 3334. The best place to eat in the neighbourhood 100m up from Haymarket Stn. 208 Bruntsfield Pl, 221 1777. In a converted church. All 7 days, lunch and dinner. LO 10/10.30pm. Cl Mon lunch. BYOB (with corkage) or unpretentious wine list. Also … **INX**

83
B1

✓ **HOWIE'S CANTEEN:** 225 5553. Glanville Pl by the br in Stockbridge. David Howie Scott's latest venture, turning a white elephant site into an instant success (maybe because they Feng Shui'd the room). Similar approach and menu to other Howies and not exactly a canteen, more a buzzy bistro with good-value contemporary food. 7 days, lunch till 4pm, LO 10pm. **INX**

84
C4
✓ **THE APARTMENT:** 228 6456. 7 Barclay Pl, up from the Kings Theatre. Contemporary eating-out experience with almost surprisingly good food, courtesy of chef Mark Lawrence in the kitchen and Malcolm Innes. You may meet Malcolm! Grazing menu and big helpings at comfortably inexp prices. Some art, some thought. An instant hit, autumn '99. This must be how to do it. Lunch Sat-Sun. Dinner 7 days, LO 11pm.   **INX**

85
B3
✓ **INDIGO YARD:** 220 5603. 7 Charlotte Lane. Food in bar area and in restau upstairs in converted and glazed-over yard behind the W End. Enormously popular and always buzzing so you may not hear your wine pop or your coin drop in the condom machine. Earlier therefore better for conversational meals, but snackier supper menu from 10pm-1am is worth remembering. Food modern Med/Mex-Scottish and better than café-bar standard. 7 days, lunch and evening menu, LO 10pm. (320/THESE ARE HIP)   **INX**

86
C4
✓ **MONTPELIERS:** 229 3115. 159 Bruntsfield Pl. Same ownership as above and similar buzz and noise levels, but more accent on food. From breakfast menu to late supper, they've thought of everything. Gets v busy. 7 days, 9am-1am, lighter menu after 10pm.   **INX**

87
C2
✓ **BROWNS:** 225 4442. 131 George St nr Charlotte Sq. First Scottish venture of this carefully-run small seventies chain, taken over for expansion by Bass. One of the most successful packaging of the late 90s Menu-U-Like, this is a reliable meal out. Huge rm can be noisy but excellent service. Quite the best of the big restaus at this end of George St. Don't even think about the others. 7 days, 10am-11.30pm (Sun open at 12noon). No booking.   **INX**

88
xE1
✓ **THE WATERFRONT:** 554 7427. 1c Dock Pl. In this foody corner of the waterfront, The Waterfront conservatory o/looks the backwater dock. It's *the* place to head in summer, but the warren of rms is cosy in winter. Food has wavered a bit over the yrs and still does, but site, setting and gr friendly service are mostly what you come for. 7 days, LO 10pm.   **MED**

89
xE1
✓ **THE SHORE:** 553 5080. 3 The Shore, Leith. Bar (often with live light jazz) where you can eat from the same menu as the dining-rm/restau. Real fire and large windows looking out to the quayside – strewn with bods on warm summer nights. Food, listed on a blackboard, changes daily but is consistently good. Lots of fish, some meat, some vegn. No smk in restau/OK in bar. 7 days, LO 10pm. (291/PUB FOOD)   **MED**

90
B3
✓ **BOUZY ROUGE:** 225 9594. 1 Alva St, nr corner with Queensferry St. Edin branch of the hugely successful bistros opened first in Airdrie, but most notably in Glas. This is well thought out accessible dining with some flair for the money (well you know what I mean). This basement can seem cramped (esp the seats), but reliable, contemporary and inexp. 7 days, lunch and dinner, LO 9.30pm (Fri-Sat 10.30pm). **INX**

91
xE1
✓ **MALMAISON BRASSERIE:** 555 6969. Tower Pl at Leith dock gates. Restau and café-bar of Malmaison (10/INDIVIDUAL HOTELS). Authentic brasserie atmos and menu, as in all Malmaisons in the expanding chain, with linen cloths, big windows, steak frites. **CAFÉ MAL** with snackier food, is less successful. 7 days. Lunch and dinner. **MED.INX**

92
D3
✓ **NICOLSON'S:** 557 4567. 6a Nicolson St, opp Festival Theatre. '99 makeover but same proprietors – they also have The Grain Store (154/SCOTTISH RESTAUS) and the coffee shop nearby (209/BEST TEAROOMS) – and vastly improved layout. Still with good window seats o/looking the theatre. Revamped menu huge improvement, esp since it's available later than most. 7 days. Lunch and dinner, LO 11pm. **MED**

93
xE1
DANIEL'S: 553 5933. 88 Commercial Quay, off Dock Pl. Versatile with small deli, takeaway and bistro. Main eaterie is housed in conservatory at back of old bonded warehouse. Clean lines, modern look and v popular. Offers contemporary French menu with Alsace and external influences that has been packing us in. Also tables by the water 7 days, 9am-10pm. **INX**

94
D3
THE DORIC: 225 1084. 15 Market St. Opp the Fruitmarket Gallery and the back entrance to Waverley Stn. Upstairs boho bistro. Recent redec though some of the old awful pictures remain. We love it anyway and always go back. Food neither remarkable nor cheap, but quintessential Edin atmos. 7 days. LO 10.30pm (and they do mean *last* orders). **MED**

95
D3
LE SEPT: 225 5428. 7 Old Fishmarket Close. The cobbled close winds steeply off the High St below St Giles. Wee o/side terr in summer and narrow woody rm inside for nonsmokers (but smokey rm too). Crêpes, omelettes, plats du jour and Franco-bistro food. Cheerful, busy rendezvous with well-regarded staff. Mon-Thu lunch and LO 10.30pm; Fri 12noon-11.30pm; Sat 12noon-11pm; Sun 12.30-10.30pm. **INX**

96
D3
THE DIAL: 225 7179. 44-46 George IV Br. Modern Scottish with an international spin in this subterranean designer eaterie. Some swear by this place, but some drawbacks, e.g. v basementy, variable service. But then it looks cool, does a bargain pre-theatre menu and much effort has gone into the aesthetics, edible or otherwise. On balance: dial their number. **MED**

97 **A ROOM IN TOWN:** 225 8204. 18 Howe St, corner of Jamaica St. No one
C2 can work out why they didn't call it 'A Room in the New Town' which is
better and describes where it is. We're not sure about the mural either.
However, good bistro menu and friendly service. 7 days, lunch and dinner.
BYOB. LO 10pm. **INX**

THE BEST FRENCH RESTAURANTS

98 ✓ **DUCK'S AT LE MARCHÉ NOIR:** 558 1608. 2-4 Eyre Pl. Malcolm
C2 Duck presides with meticulous attention to detail in his bistro/restau
at the lower end of the New Town. In a residential neighbourhood, an
easy-going but still business-like atmos. Various *menus complets*, with
some imaginative regional variations and regular gourmet evenings.
Good-value wine list. Dinner 7 days, lunch Mon-Fri. LO 10.30pm (earlier
Sun). **MED**

99 ✓ **CAFÉ SAINT-HONORÉ:** 226 2211. 34 Thistle St Lane, betw Frederick
C2 St and Hanover St. Suits a-plenty, New Town regulars and occasional
lunching ladies all to be found in this busy, shiny bistro-cum-restau where
menu smacks of *fin de siècle* Paris. No starving artists or bohemians – just
a *fin de 20th siècle* restau with a distinct French flavour. Veggies should
phone ahead. **EXP**

100 ✓ **BISTRO PROVENÇALE:** 229 4404. 21 Argyle Pl. Authentic corner de
xD4 France in Marchmont's main st. Could be Montparnasse. Straight
talking menu has some French flair. Even frog's legs and fondue on Tue.
Cheap cheap lunch. BYOB. Cl Sun-Mon. **INX**

101 ✓ **JACQUES:** 229 6080. 8 Gillespie Pl, Bruntsfield. Endearing French staff
xC4 and atmos. Hard-working wee rustic eaterie close to the King's Theatre.
Has all those French dishes – mussels, roulade – and throws in left-fielders
like ostrich, yes, ostrich! Loyal following, you may need to book. Also Sun
brunch. Lunch and LO 11pm Mon-Sat, 10am-10pm Sun. **INX**

102 ✓ **BONARS:** 556 5888. 58 St Mary's St. The Bonars moved from their
C2 highly-regarded country restau in Gifford to take over this once formal eaterie. Still a sense that *beurre* wouldn't melt in the mouth, but some

dishes are quite inspired. When the new Parliament opens round the corner, intrigue may add more piquancy to the sauce. 7 days (though may be closed Sun, so check) lunch and dinner. LO 9.30pm. **EXP**

103
C2
✓ **CHAMBERTIN:** 225 1251. 21 George St. Discreet, v professionally run main restau of George Hotel (9/BEST HOTELS) in opulent salon where suits dine at lunch time and other members of the Edin establishment compare chips (on the shoulder). More relaxed in the evenings. Food more *au courant* than previously. Lunch Mon-Fri, LO 10pm Mon-Sat. Cl Sun. **EXP**

104
D4
LA BONNE VIE: 667 1110. 49 Causewayside. Popular bistro in Edin's Southside. V agreeable. Sitting among the garlands, stone walls, shining glassware and candles for a few mins, there's a growing sense of personality, then it hits you. This is the Felicity Kendall of capital restaus – and that's a compliment. Scottish produce, French outlook. Lunch and LO 10.30pm daily. **MED**

105
D3
PIERRE VICTOIRE: 225 1721. 10 Victoria St. For those who followed the rise and fall of Pierre Levicky who created the Pierre Victoire 'cheap, cheerful … and authentic' bistro chain, took over the world and then, suddenly went under, this place is of some interest. It was his first venture. There are others in town, all privately managed – this is still the one to try. 7 days. Lunch and dinner. LO 10.30pm. **INX**

106
D1
BLEU: 557 8451. 4 Union St. The branch we prefer (less claustrophobic) of this 'new concept' former Pierre Victoire. *Bouchées* are mouthfuls, like tapas, but helpings are huge so food is a gr deal. Other branches in Stockbridge (8 Gloucester St, 225 1037) and Victoria St (226 1900). 7 days, lunch and dinner. **INX**

107
C2
LA P'TITE FOLIE 225 7983. 61 Frederick St. Formerly Chez Jules. The word is unpretentious – mismatched furniture, inexp French *plat du jour*. Cheap lunch. 7 days. Cl Sun lunch. **INX**

108
B2
CAFÉ D'ODILE: 225 5366. 13 Randolph Cres. A secret grd and small cafeteria downstairs at the French Institute. Lunch only but can be booked for parties at night. Gr views over the New Town, simple French home-cooking, patronized by ladies who lunch and students. BYOB. Tue-Sat. **CHP**

LA POTINIÈRE: 01620 843214. Main St, Gullane. Report: 66/BEST RESTAUS.

THE VINTNER'S ROOM: 554 6767. 87 Giles St, Leith. Report: 74/BEST RESTAUS.

THE BEST ITALIAN RESTAURANTS

109
B3
✓ **SCALINI:** 220 2999. 10 Melville Pl. Downstairs (the *scalini*) bistro restau in a low-ceilinged sliver of a basement with a straightforward and personal approach to Italian cooking – Silvio will tell you what's good tonight and he'll be right. They have an amazing collection of vintage Barolos and other excellent wine, probably one for your birthday. Smoking upstairs. Cl Sun. **MED**

110
E1
✓ **VALVONA & CROLLA:** 556 6066. 19 Elm Row. Café at the back of the legendary deli, and with all the flair and attention to detail that you would expect. First-class ingredients, produce shipped in from Italy (fresh veg from Milan markets) and gr Italian domestic cooking. This place is a treat without the trappings. Everything from vegn breakfast to fab lemon polenta cake and coffee for afternoon nibblers via a damned fine lunch. May be queues. No smk. Mon-Sat 8am-5pm. Not cheap, but who's counting the lira? **INX**

111
C2
✓ **COSMO:** 226 6743. 58 N Castle St (a no through rd). V much in the old, discreet style for those with some time and cash on their hands. In Edin terms, has been the up-market Italian restau for yrs and it is often fully booked. Famous people like Sean do get brought here. The lighting and the music are soft, the service impeccable and the (Italian) wine list exemplary. Menu pragmatically brief; allow time to enjoy it. 6 days. Cl Sun and Sat lunch. **EXP**

112
xE2
✓ **TINELLI:** 652 1932. 139 Easter Rd. Small and neat restau with unassuming frontage on unfashionable st that was serving air-dried beef long before anyone else. Many fans swear by it! Not a pizza/pasta joint – grilled liver with balsamic vinegar more their style. One of the city's best Italians. Lunch and LO 10.30pm Mon-Sat. **MED**

113
B3
✓ **BAR ROMA:** 226 2977. 39 Queensferry St. One of Edin's long-standing fave Italians, now revamped and hurtled into the 90s. Almost looks like a Pizza Express from the o/side. Inside always bustling (this includes the menu) with real Italian rude waiters as the floor show. 7 days, all day. LO 11.30pm. **INX**

114
C2
EST EST EST: 225 2555. 135 George St at W End. Though my own feeling about this place (the food) is ugh, ugh, ugh, there's no question that it works in a super-restau way. Busy, noisy, sleek and modern – it's a New

Labour kinda thing. Food and service – who cares? The people say yes. 7 days. LO 11pm. **INX**

115
C1
TONY'S: 226 5877. 42 St Stephen St. Identifiable by the floral window box, this small tratt features a high standard of Italian cooking, comparable with the standard of patter from Tony himself. V popular so book. Daily, evenings only, LO 11pm. Slightly larger **TONY'S** at 19 Colinton Rd, 447 8781. Same menu, excellent service. **INX**

116
A4
PEPE'S TAVERNA: 337 9774. 96 Dalry Rd. Taverna's just the word – checked tablecloths, dark wooden fixtures and hanging pots and pans. Food is standard Italian but when virtually everywhere else has packed up for the night, Pepe's keeps on keeping on. A Dalry haven 6pm-2.30am. Cl Tue. (241/LATE-NIGHT RESTAUS) **INX**

117
D2
GIULIANO'S: 556 6590. 18 Union Pl, top of Leith Walk nr the main r/bout, opp Playhouse Theatre. No change at Giuli's but something sets it apart as it's usually heaving with happy punters, many birthdays! It's just pasta and pizza but in a no-nonsense menu that appeals. The food is great, the din is loud. Lunch and LO 2am daily. Also another 'on the shore' in Leith (554 5272) which is esp good for kids (192/KID-FRIENDLY). **INX**

UMBERTO'S: 554 1314. Off Bonnington Rd. Report: 190/KID-FRIENDLY.

GORDON'S TRATTORIA: 225 7992. 231 High St. Report: 239/LATE-NIGHT RESTAUS.

THE BEST PIZZA

118
B1
✓ **PIZZA EXPRESS:** 332 7229. 1 Deanhaugh St, Stockbridge. Burgeoning national chain, same formula everywhere, but what-the-hell, it's great pizza (and ambience). Stockbridge branch best, in refurbed bank with Water of Leith gurgling below. Simple, no-nonsense, affordable pizza with good service. Award for architecture. Edin W End branch, 225 8863, 32 Queensferry St. Both open till 12midnight daily. Also North Br, adj Carlton Highland Hotel, but these 2 branches best vibes. No booking.
INX

119
E1
JOLLY: 556 1588. 9 Elm Row. The original, unaltered '70s pizza point with wood-burning oven. Frilly, democratic and no irony – but gr pizzas and gr service. Mon-Sat and LO 11.30pm, Sun 4-10.30pm.
INX

120
C3
MAMMA'S: 225 6464. 30 Grassmarket. Brash, American-style with informal booking system (chalk your name on the board then nip off to the pub to wait). Some alternatives to pizza, but you come to mix 'n' match – haggis, calamari and BBQ sauce and 40 other toppings. 12noon-10.30pm Sun-Thu, till 1am Fri-Sat (later if you're still eating). Also 1 Howard St, Canonmills.
INX

121
xE1
CAPRICE: 554 1279. 325-331 Leith Walk. Old-style – hip in the '70s but bought over a few years back and not quite what it was. But – wood-burning oven, packed with Leithers at peak times; the pizza's fine. Lunch Mon-Sat, LO 11pm Mon-Thu, 11.30pm Fri-Sat, 10pm Sun.
INX

122
A4
MARIO'S: 337 6711. 105 Dalry Rd. Well-kept secret in this not so up-market part of town (1 km Haymarket Stn) with loyal clientele – Mario knows 90% of his customers by name. Good for kids, gr for pizza. Lunch and LO 10pm (Fri-Sat 11.30pm).
INX

THE BEST RESTAURANTS FOR MEDITERRANEAN FOOD

123
D3
✓ **IGG'S:** 557 8184. 15 Jeffrey St, nr Royal Mile. Maybe misleading to include Igg's here because although it serves the best tapas in town, they're only available at lunch. Overall, it's a v smart eaterie serving some of the best victuals in Edin – Spanish/Scots crossover. Excellent sauces and riojas. People in the know eat here. Lunch, LO 10.30pm. Cl Sun. **MED**

124
D3
✓ **BARIOJA:** 557 3622. 19 Jeffrey St. And along from Iggs (*see above*), a tapas bar – they are joined together in the basement. Small tables and not much room to move upstairs; more space, less ambience down. Sound, authentic tapas menu, though no piled counters like Spain. 11am-11pm. Cl Sun. **INX**

125
D2
✓ **MEDITERRANEO:** 557 6900. 73 Broughton St. Fairly discreet frontage on busy little Broughton St. Family feel (the Crollas, scions of the Valvona and Crolla) to this café/bistro/restau serving not unsurprisingly Mediterranean snacks and meals, but not pasta. Deli counter, various coffee. 7 days lunch and Thu-Sat dinner, LO 9.30pm. **INX.MED**

126
D2
✓ **TAPAS TREE:** 556 7118. 1 Forth St. Bustling wee restau with upbeat Spanish staff and gypsy/Cajun soundtrack. Starter/main/pud is the heavier option but 3 well-chosen tapas (veg, fish and something else) with some robust bread and a bottle of house red makes for a v decent meal. Snappy service. This place unusual in that it gets better and better. Tapas in the £2 to £5 range, so not a pocket-buster. 11am-10.30pm daily. **INX**

127
D4
PHENECIA: 662 4493. 55-57 W Nicolson St, on corner nr Edin Univ. Unfussy yellow N African/Spanish eaterie with couscous, lots of grilled meats and wide vegn choice. Poss to eat v cheaply at lunch-time – some people just pop in from that univ for hummus and salad. Lunch Mon-Sat, LO 11pm daily (10pm Sun). They have the Château Musar. **INX**

128
C2
TAPAS OLÉ: 556 2754, 8-10 Eyre Pl and 225 7069, 4 Forrest Rd, nr the Univ. Tapas restau/bar. Meat/vegn/seafood menus and the usual vinos. Spacious rather than cosy with Spanish proprietor and waiters. Live music on Sun. 7 days, lunch and LO 10.30 pm. **INX**

THE BEST SEAFOOD RESTAURANTS

129
xE1

✓ ✓ **SKIPPERS:** 554 1018. 1a Dock Pl, Leith. Bistro with truly maritime atmos; mainly seafood. Best to book. Many would argue Skippers *is* the best place to eat seafood in town. Full report: 80/BEST BISTROS.

130
xE1

✓ ✓ **FISHERS:** 554 5666. Corner of The Shore and Tower St, Leith. At the foot of an 18th-century tower opp Malmaison Hotel and rt on the quay (though no boats come by). Seafood cooking with flair and commitment in boat-like surroundings where trad Scots dishes get an imaginative twist. Hugely popular, some stools around bar and tables o/side in summer (can be a windy corner). Often all are packed. Cheeseboard has some gr Brits if you have rm for a third course. 7 days. 12noon-10.30pm. **MED**

131
D3

CREELERS: 220 4447. 3 Hunter Sq. Tim and Fran James still holding on to their excellent seafood restau and smokehouse in Arran, also called Creelers. But they're mainly to be found in this corner of the revamped Hunter Sq behind the Tron Church, just a short cast from the Royal Mile (tables alfresco in summer). One of the best seafood spots in town. Nice paintings, good atmos, not exp. Bar meals at front, restau at back. Lunch and LO 10.30/11pm (cl Sun in winter). **MED**

132
C2

THE MUSSEL INN: 225 5979. 61 Rose St. In the heart of the city centre where parking ain't easy, a gr little seafood bistro specializing in mussels and scallops (kings and queens) which the proprietors rear/find themselves. Also 'catch of the day' and a non-fish pasta option. Good chips. Lunch and dinner. Cl Sun-Mon. LO 10pm. **INX**

133
D2

CAFÉ ROYAL OYSTER BAR: 556 4124. W Register St. 'Under new management', still a place for a flourish of insanity or sheer exhibitionism. Beluga caviar followed by Homard Newburg with a bottle of Bolly will cost you an arm and a leg. But you can also snack. Higher celeb quotient there for the classy surroundings with spillover atmos from adj bar. Tiles, linen, dark wood, v Victorian. Visitors usually find it all v groovy; locals lament that it ain't what it was. Lunch and LO 10.15pm daily. **EXP**

134
D4

LA BONNE MER: 662 9111. 113 Buccleuch St, nr the Univ. Discreet, some would say, tidy little seafood bistro. On a site which has seen many different cuisines in the past, this time it seems to work. Food simple, prices esp inexp; 'student' 2-course lunch £5. BYOB. Tue-Sat, lunch and LO 10pm. Related to **LA BONNE VIE** (104/FRENCH RESTAUS). **INX**

THE BEST FISH 'N' CHIPS

135
C1 ✓ **L'ALBA D'ORO:** Henderson Row, nr corner with Dundas St. Large selection of deep-fried goodies, incl many vegn savouries. Inexp proper pasta, real pizzas and even the wine's OK. A lot more than your usual fry-up – as several plaques on the wall attest (incl *Scotland the Best!*). Open till 12midnight. **CHP**

136
D2 ✓ **THE RAPIDO:** 77 Broughton St. Fine chips. Popular with late-nighters stumbling back down the hill to the New Town, and the flotsam of the 'Pink Triangle'. Open till 1.30am (3.30am Fri-Sat). **CHP**

137
D2 ✓ **THE DEEP SEA:** Leith Walk, opp Playhouse. Open late and often has queues but these are quickly dispatched. The haddock has to be 'of a certain size'. Trad menu. Still one of the best fish suppers you'll ever feed a hangover with. Open till 2am (-ish) (3am Fri-Sat). **CHP**

THE BEST VEGETARIAN RESTAURANTS

138
D4
✓ **SUSIE'S DINER:** 667 8729. 51-53 W Nicolson St. Cosy, neighbourhood (univ) self-service diner. Nice people behind and in front of the counter. Mexican and Middle-Eastern dishes, occasional live music and belly dancing nights. Licensed, also BYOB. Mon 9am-8pm, Tue-Sat 9am-10pm. Cl Sun. **CHP**

139
D3
✓ **BANNS:** 226 1112. 5 Hunter Sq, just off Royal Mile at the Tron Church. Veggie burgers, Mexicana and many less predictable things in this informal eaterie on a redeveloped corner of the Old Town; tables o/side in summer. Snacks and full meals all day, some vegan. Organic wines and beers, decent coffee from Gaggia machine. Daily 10am-11pm. **INX**

140
C2
✓ **HENDERSON'S:** 225 2131. 94 Hanover St. Edin's original and trailblazing basement vegn self-serve café-cum-wine bar. Canteen seating to the left (avoid) and candles and live piano or guitar downstairs to the rt (better). Happy wee wine list and bottles of some excellent organic real ales. Good cheese. Cl Sun. LO 10pm. Also has the Farm Shop upstairs with a deli and takeaway and the more bar-like **HENDERSON'S THISTLE BISTRO** round the corner in Thistle St and a **TAKEAWAY IN CANONMILLS**, nr the clock with tables (some hot dishes). NOTE: Henderson's organic oatcakes are *the* best. **CHP**

141
D3
✓ **BLACK BO'S:** 557 6136. 57 Blackfriars St. Unlike other eateries below, this is a restau, not a way of life. You could just about bring your meaty boyfriend here. Not precious, not perfect, but good vegn ideas and combos. Woody, laid-back set-up. Adj bar has been cool for yrs. Food less fruity than formerly and not so stodgy. 7 days, not Sun lunch. LO 10.30pm. **INX**

142
D4
✓ **KALPNA:** 667 9890. 2-3 St Patrick Sq. Ingredients taken seriously in this long-established vegn restau which is also something else – a good Indian one – so more interesting than many. Thali gives a good overview while bargain Wed buffet features regional cuisine. No smk. Lunch Mon-Fri, dinner Mon-Sat, LO 10.30pm. (164/INDIAN RESTAUS) **INX**

143
D4
✓ **ANN PURNA:** 662 1807. 45 St Patrick Sq. Excellent vegn restau nr Edin Univ with genuine Gujerati/S Indian cuisine. Good atmos – old customers are greeted like friends. Indian beer, some suitable wines. Lunch Mon-Fri, dinner 7 days, LO 11pm. (165/INDIAN RESTAUS) **INX**

144 **ENGINE SHED CAFÉ:** 662 0040. 19 St Leonard's Lane. Hidden away off St
E4 Leonard's St, this is a lunch-oriented vegn café where much of the work is
done by adults with learning difficulties on training placements, so worth
supporting. Simple, decent food and gr bread – baked on premises, for
sale separately. Nice stopping-off point after a tramp over Arthur's Seat
(366/BEST WALKS). (Also has a shop at 123 Bruntsfield Pl.) Mon-Thu
10.30am-3.30pm, Fri 10.30am-2.30pm, Sat 10.30am-4pm, Sun 11.30am-
4pm. **CHP**

145 **HELIOS FOUNTAIN:** 229 7884. 7 Grassmarket. Old hippies eat sugar-free
C3 cake, their kids play with building blocks and browsers check out the
tenets of Steinerism (Rudolf, not George). Reliable self-service vegn caff,
anthroposophical bookshop and gewgaw emporium. No smk. Mon-Sat
10am-6pm, Sun 12noon-5pm. **CHP**

146 **CORNERSTONE CAFÉ:** 229 0212. Underneath St John's Church at the
C3 corner of Princes St and Lothian Rd. V central and PC self-service coffee
shop in church vaults. Home-baking and hot dishes at lunchtime. Some
seats o/side in summer (in graveyard!) and market stalls during the
Festival. One World Shop adj is full of Third World-type crafts and v good
for presents. A respite from the fast-food frenzy and money round of
Princes St. Open 9.30am-5pm (later in Festival). Cl Sun. **CHP**

147 **ISABEL'S:** 662 4014. 83 Clerk St (in basement of Nature's Gate wholefood
E4 shop). V small café selling vegn standards. Pop in some time. Mon-Sat
11.30am-6.30pm. (Cl earlier Tue and Sat.) **CHP**

THE BEST SCOTTISH RESTAURANTS

148
C2

✓ **WINTER GLEN:** 477 7060. 3a1 Dundas St, which is on the rt going downhill opp the Scottish Gallery. Comfortable, intimate basement restau. Pleasing name comes not from sentiment, but from the surnames of the owners. Nevertheless this mainly Scottish menu originates from glen and loch and bay; Scotland's first-class ingredients featured and presented to exemplary effect. Smart service, urbane atmos. In most of the other guides too (though only 1 AA rosette). 6 days. Cl Sun. **MED**

149
D3

✓ **DUBH PRAIS:** 557 5732. 123b High St. Slap bang (but downstairs) on the Royal Mile opp the Holiday Inn. Only 9 tables and a miniature galley kitchen from which proprietor/chef James McWilliams and his team produce a remarkably reliable à la carte menu from sound and sometimes surprising Scottish ingredients. Remarkable and surprising because you might not expect the largely suburban clientele to feast so enthusiastically on ostrich or rabbit, but they do. Testimony to the chef; there are many more conventional options. An outpost of culinary integrity on the Royal Mile. Cl Sun-Mon. LO 10.30pm. **MED**

150
D2

HALDANE'S: 556 8407. 39 Albany St. In basement of The Albany (18/INDIVIDUAL HOTELS). Fine dining nr Broughton St and prob the best meal in the area. Scottish by nature rather than hype. Everything done in a country house style, down to the bar snacks. Lunch Mon-Fri, LO 9.30pm daily. **MED**

151
D3

OFF THE WALL: 667 1597. 11 S College St, nr Univ and round corner from Festival Theatre (hence inexp pre and aprés 'theatre menu'). Not so much off the wall as in the wall, a discreet bistro often missed by the ravening foodies (but not Gillian Glover of *Scotland on Sunday* who loved it … and if it's good enough for her …). Short, simple menu with all the Scottish stalwarts (salmon, venison, beef) all nicely concocted with contemporary ingredients and twist. Mon-Sat, lunch and LO 10pm or later by arrangement. **MED**

152
D3

JACKSONS: 225 1793. 209 High St. In the midst of the Mile, Jacksons plays the Scottish card big time. Here for over 15 yrs, this is a v Taste of Scotland experience. In the cellar so to speak, but tables o/side in summer. Not sure about the haggis timbale thing, but Lyn MacKinnon I like and she's so … well, very Scottish. 7 days, lunch and dinner. **MED**

153
C3, D2

STAC POLLY: 229 5405. 8a Grindlay St. Opp Lyceum Theatre and not far from Usher Hall, Traverse and cinemas. Those haggis filo parcels that divide opinion are still on the menu which is largely local produce cooked up a storm (Scottish beef, salmon, game). The restau – dark wood and tartan curtains – is quietly smart. Cheeses come from Iain Mellis. There's another basement **STAC POLLY** at 29-33 Dublin St in the New Town (556 2231). Similar menu but it feels clubbier. V fine. Both: lunch Mon-Fri (Sat lunch at Dublin St). Dinner 7 days, LO 10/11pm (Grindlay St later). **MED**

154
D3

THE GRAIN STORE: 225 7635. 30 Victoria St. Regulars climb the stairs for the pigeon, salmon or guinea fowl – perhaps the vegn alternative – then hang around this laid-back first-floor eaterie drinking wine or coffee. Informal and welcoming, there are few better places for a relaxed Sun lunch extending far into the afternoon. Perhaps more 'mod Brit' than simply 'Scottish'. Lunch and dinner daily. LO 11pm, though much earlier Mon-Thu, so check. **MED**

155
xE4

FENWICK'S: 667 4265. 15 Salisbury Pl. Tucked away in the depths of Newington, though with plenty students and tourists from the drab hotel belt to attract, this 90s kind of restau is an honest-to-goodness treat. Excellent value. The cooking, with assorted international manoeuvres, offers local produce turned out with a goodly degree of style and honesty. Affordable wine list chalked up on the wall, but can BYOB. Lunch and LO 10.30pm. **INX**

THE BEST MEXICAN (AND CENTRAL AMERICAN) RESTAURANTS

156
D3

✓ **VIVA MEXICO:** 226 5145. Anchor Close, Cockburn St. Has it really been here more than a dozen yrs? That says something about its position among the come-and-go Mexicans. Still throws in something innovative now and again, although all the expected dishes are here. Reliable venue for those times when nothing else fits the mood but sour cream, tacos and limey lager; nice atmos downstairs. Another branch nr Tollcross at 50 E Fountainbridge. Lunch (not Sun) and LO 10.30pm. **INX**

157
E4

✓ **MOTHER'S:** 662 0772. 107-109 St Leonard's St. Gr wee neighbourhood restau that manages to do the basics well (unlike many other Tex/Mexicans in town). Burgers, beef, burritos and one or two departures like Cajun veggie kebabs. Simple décor, good staff, proper coffee, homemade desserts. A hit, a palpable hit. Dinner 6-10pm Tue-Thu and Sun, 6-10.30pm Fri-Sat. Cl Mon. **INX**

158
C2

TEX MEX: 225 1796. 47 Hanover St. Young, dumb and full of, er, tequila. A Primal Scream of a place in the city centre with all the usual Mexican faves, José Cuervo experiments and jolly soundtrack. Probably the best appointed of its ilk in Edin; infinitely preferable to others nearby. Slammersville. 12noon-1am Mon-Sat, till 12midnight Sun. **INX**

159
E3

PANCHO VILLAS: 557 4416. 240 Canongate. This spartan cantina remains a reliable exponent of what we've come to regard as Mexican cooking with nosh of the 'chilada, 'ajita, 'ichanga school. Plain décor, decent edibles, happy place for parties. Lunch 12noon-2.30pm Mon-Sat, dinner 6-10.30pm daily. **INX**

160
B3

CUBA NORTE: 221 1430. Morrison St (W End nr Haymarket Stn). Yes, we know it's not Mexican and perhaps not Cuban either, but this bar/restau with Latin vibes has been a success since it opened late '98 (despite the pundits poo-pooing that a cool place could be this far W). Bar at front, tables upstairs through back serving Cuba-style cuisine (though we know they don't have any food, never mind a cuisine, over there). More Miami than Malecon. Some tango, flamenco and DJ salsa (various w/end nights) may drown out the flava later on, but a better attempt at Havana than others. 7 days lunch and LO 10.30pm. **INX**

THE BEST INDIAN RESTAURANTS

161
D3

✓ **SURUCHI:** 556 6583. 14a Nicolson St. Upstairs opp Festival Theatre. Owner from Jaipur called Mr Rodriguez plus chefs from Bengal, Delhi and S India equals eclectic Indian menu. Unfussy décor and food with light touch (good coconut rice) attracts students/academics from nearby univ as well as theatregoers. This place is routinely praised to the skies; mostly we agree. Live music some nights. Lunch and LO 11.30pm daily.

INX

162
D3

✓ **KEBAB MAHAL:** 667 5214. 7 Nicolson Sq. Nr Edin Univ and Festival Theatre. Gr vegetable biryani and delicious lassi for under a fiver? Hence high cult status. Late-night Indo-Pakistani halal caff that attracts Asian families as well as students and others who know. Kebabs, curries and excellent sweets. One of Edin's most cosmopolitan restaus. Sun-Thu 12noon-12midnight, Fri-Sat 12noon-2am. No alcohol baby! **CHP**

163
xE1

✓ **THE RAJ:** 553 3980. 89 Henderson St on S corner of The Shore, Leith. Take a certain amount of care with the food, add Tommy Miah's marketing nous and wadda-you-get? The most successful Indian/Bangladeshi restau in town. Regular events (Bangladeshi New Year and Food/Culture Fest) add to the jollity; jars of things available to buy and take home, also recipe books. Sun-Thu still does food 'at 1983 prices'. Try to sit up on the raised front area – better than the back. Totally Raj, in the non-Irvine Welsh sense (in-joke for Edin readers). Lunch and LO 11.30pm, 7 days. **CURRY IN A HURRY:** 0800 073 1983. Get the Raj menu delivered (3 mile radius), evenings only. **INX**

164
D4

KALPNA: 667 9890. 2-3 St Patrick Sq. The original Edin Indian veggie restau and still ragingly popular. Lighter, fluffier and not as attritional as so many tandooris. Wed buffet a bargain. Report: 142/VEGN RESTAUS. **INX**

165
D4

ANN PURNA: 662 1807. 45 St Patrick Sq. Friendly and family-run Gujerati/S Indian veggie restau with seriously value-for-money business lunch. Report: 143/VEGN RESTAUS. **INX**

166
C1

LANCERS: 332 3444. 5 Hamilton Pl. Bengali/N Indian, off busy Hamilton Pl in Stockbridge/New Town area. A 'Brits in India, those were the days' type restau which can mean service on the precious side, but the food speaks for itself. Dining area not so comfortable, but New Townies with lovely kitchens do phone for a kerry-oot. 7 days. LO 11pm. **INX**

167 **INDIAN CAVALRY CLUB:** 228 3282. Athol Pl, W End, just off the main
B3 Glas rd, about 250m from Princes St. Bargain business lunch attracts the
suits. Another restau you'll like if you go for the retro colonial style. We
don't esp – but no quibbles about the nibbles or the mainly excellent
main dishes. This seems an unlikely carry-out place, but they do, and it's
one of the best in town. Lunch and LO 11.30pm daily.   **INX**

168 **SHAMIANA:** 228 2265. 14 Brougham St, Tollcross. Recommended by
C4 everyone from Egon Ronay (not a recommendation we'd rely on) to
Gordon Brown our dear Treasurer. Over 20 yrs in this spot and once the
most stylish and reliably good. Now more one of many, but only exclu-
sively N Indian/Kashmiri cuisine in town. Open curiously short hrs, dinner
only. Closes (not LO) 10.15pm (9pm Sun, i.e. only open 3 hrs).   **MED**

169 **KUSHI'S:** 556 8996. 16 Drummond St. Long regarded as the only real
D3 Indian, this basic Punjabi café (no restau twiddly bits) has been drawing
in students and others for cheap eats since Nehru was in his collar, or at
least in the news. It's just round the corner from Edin Univ's Old College.
Short no-nonsense menu, cheap no-nonsense prices. Unique, this is the
stripped-down curry. Lunch Mon-Sat, dinner Mon-Thu 5-8.30pm, Fri-Sat
5-9.30pm. Cl Sun.   **CHP**

THE BEST FAR-EASTERN RESTAURANTS

170 ✓ **ERAWAN ORIENTAL:** 556 4242. 14 S St Andrews St. The latest and
D2 most upmarket part of the dynasty (*see below*), betw Princes St and
the soon-to-come Harvey Nix. Location the thing, but large brasserie-type
rm with competent Thai cuisine mainly business at lunch and pleasure at
night. Prob the best Thai in town. 7 days. LO 11pm.   **INX**

171 **SIAM ERAWAN:** 226 3675. 48 Howe St. On corner of Stockbridge area,
C2 the first proper Thai in town and still rated – manages that quiet Eastern
elegance v well. Same people also have **ERAWAN EXPRESS**, 220 0059,
176 Rose St, a kind of Thai canteen but not quite as inspired as its big sis.
Both establishments lunch Mon-Sat, dinner daily, LO 11pm.   **INX**

172
D3, C4
AYUTTHAYA: 556 9351. 14b Nicolson St, opp Festival Theatre. Decent prospect pre- or post-show. Long, thin, not atmos restau, but attentive service, good vegn selection and a steady hand in the kitchen. Under the same ownership is **SUKHOTHAI:** 229 1537. 23 Brougham Pl, Tollcross. Funkier eaterie where the waitresses do their best to look delicate but would perhaps feel better in baseball caps. Sip your Singha – think not of Phuket. LO 10pm. **INX**

173
B3
YUMI: 337 2173. 2 W Coates (continues from Haymarket Terr, W End). The classier and more polite of the capital's Japanese restaus. Our researcher thought it the cleanest rip in town. Still Michelin awards 2 forks. One day when we are loaded, we'll be back. Go if you must have sushi. Dinner only. LO 11pm. Cl Sun. **EXP**

174
C2
TAMPOPO: 220 5254. 25a Thistle St. Not a restau at all but a gr wee Japanese noodle bar where you can pick up a ramen to go or one of those meal-on-a-tray things. Open lunch Mon-Sat, also 6-9pm Tue-Sat. Cl Sun. **CHP**

THE WOK BAR: 667 8594. 30 Rottenrow. Report: 301/PUB FOOD.

THE BEST CHINESE RESTAURANTS

175
C2
✓ **KWEILIN:** 557 1875. 19 Dundas St. Large New Town place with imaginative Cantonese cooking (real chefs); v good seafood and genuine dim sum in pleasant but somewhat uninspired setting. No kids allowed in the evening – somewhere for grown-ups to eat their quail in peace. Book. LO 10.45pm. Cl Sun-Mon. **MED**

176
xE4
✓ **DRAGON WAY:** 668 1328. 74 S Clerk St. First thing that hits you as you go in – a big lacquer dragon wrapped around a pillar. Décor gloriously OTT and often described as 'Hollywood film set'. Good food mind you, and service, so one of the more interesting Chinese nights out. Lunch Mon-Fri and LO 12midnight. **INX**

177
C3
✓ **ORIENTAL DINING CENTRE:** 221 1288. 8 Morrison St, opp cinema complex. It's a restau (**RAINBOW ARCH**), a dim sum basement bar and a late-night noodle shack (**HOHOMEI** – cash only, eat in or take-

away). Noodles 5.30pm-2.30am Mon-Sat. The restau is best by far in this neck of the W End. 12noon-12midnight daily. **INX**

178
xE1
✓ **YEE KIANG:** 554 5833. 42 Dalmeny St. Authentic Chinese home cooking courtesy of Michael Wong deep in the heart of Hibbie land – recent refurb but feels like someone's living rm. Small, democratic. Does the real Chinese tea ceremony. An inside track choice. 7 days, 5.30-10.30pm (11.30pm w/ends). **INX**

179
B3
✓ **LUNE TOWN:** 220 1688. 38 William St. The wee one hidden away behind the W End. A classy Chinese, often busy. Predominantly Cantonese cuisine. Lunch and LO 11.30pm Mon-Fri. Open 3pm-12midnight Sat-Sun. **MED**

180
C1
✓ **LOON FUNG:** 556 1781. 2 Warriston Pl, Canonmills. Upstairs (and down when it's crowded) the famous lemon chicken and crispy duck go round for ever. And damned fine seaweed. Lunch and LO 11.30pm (Sun-Thu), 12.30am (Fri-Sat). **INX**

181
B3
NEW EDINBURGH RENDEZVOUS: 225 2023. 10a Queensferry St. Hardly new and easy to miss (upstairs, next door to travel agents). Functional décor, short wine list to be taken seriously and dishes you won't find in any other Scottish Chinese restaus, e.g. shredded sea blubber. Sound nice? Well this restau is for diehards. They'd say nobody does better Peking food in this town. 7 days. Lunch and LO 11pm Mon-Sat, 1-11pm Sun. **INX**

182
C4
LEE ON: 229 7732. 3-5 Bruntsfield Pl. Through purple porthole-effect windows, a restau popular with the Chinese community. Feels a bit *Man From UNCLE*, but food fine. 7 days. Lunch and dinner. LO 12midnight. **INX**

THE BEST RESTAURANTS FOR BURGERS AND STEAKS

183
xA2
✓ ✓ **CHAMPANY'S:** 01506 834532. On A904, Linlithgow to S Queensferry rd (3km Linlithgow), but nr M9 at jnct 3. Accolade-laden restau (and 'Chop and Ale House') different from others below because it's out of town (and out of some pockets). Both surf 'n' turf with

live lobsters on premises. Good service, huge helpings (Americans may feel at home). Chop House 7 days, lunch and LO 10pm; restau lunch (not Sat) and LO 10pm. Cl Sun. Hotel rms adj (52/HOTELS O/SIDE TOWN). **INX.EXP**

184
C1
BELL'S DINER: 225 8116. 7 St Stephen St, Stockbridge. Bill Allan will understand why I can't say anything more about this legendary American diner. Nothing has changed in 20 yrs except the annual paint job. Burgers, steaks, shakes and coincidentally, the best veggie (nut) burger in town. Mon-Fri 6-10.30pm, Sat-Sun 12noon-10.30pm. **INX**

185
xE4
BANKS: 667 0707. 10 Newington Rd. 2-floor restau on Southside nr Univ and Meadows. Downstairs is excellent value grill rm with real chef (Peter Banks) on the stove. Best chips in town? Gr desserts. Report: 77/BEST RESTAUS. **INX.MED**

186
xE1
THE ROCK: 555 2225. Commercial St, Leith. Where to go for lunch with clients or dinner out when all you want is a decent steak/burger (there are other options). Best in Leith, with Bell's the best in town, and the most up-market on this page. Poss changes in 2000. Report: 78/BEST RESTAUS. **MED**

187
D4, B1
BUFFALO GRILL: 667 7427. 12-14 Chapel St and 1 Raeburn Pl, Stockbridge (332 3864). Burn that beef! Although this diner trades on its reputation for steaks and such-like, there are some Mexican concessions to veggies. Book and BYOB. Lunch Mon-Fri, LO 10.15pm (Sun 10pm). **INX**

188
D4
SMOKE STACK: 556 6032. 53-55 Broughton St. From the makers of The Basement (262/GR EDIN PUBS) came something across the rd – a burgundy and blue diner rather than an orange and blue bar. Modish décor has a soothing effect. Loads of burgers (Scottish beef or vegn), seared salmon, etc. jollied along by a gr staff. (Santana at lunch time, old times/new times.) Proper menu available lunch and dinner, but food of some sort all day. Also does a good Sun brunch (248/SUN BREAKFAST). Open 12noon-10.30pm daily. **INX**

189
C2
WIGWAM: 225 6127. 64 Thistle St. Bright colours in this central, but back-street Native Americana diner. Mainly meat – a buffalo wings kinda joint – but vegn burgers too, with a good guacamole. Tex-Mex obviously, handy business lunch venue. Lunch and LO 11pm daily. **INX**

KID-FRIENDLY PLACES

190
xE1

✓ **UMBERTO'S:** 554 1314. Bonnington Rd Lane off Bonnington Rd to E of Newhaven Rd jnct. Whitewashed coach house hidden away in a v unlikely part of Leith. In contrast to some other 'kiddie' places, grown-ups would actually want to eat here too. Downstairs is a civilized restau, upstairs a theme area for kids where some booths form part of a big toy train and mobile youngsters can run in and out of the Wendy house. Excellent Italian cooking with a Scottish twist. Upstairs open Mon-Fri 12noon-2pm then 5-7.30pm, Sat 12noon-7.30pm, Sun 12noon-5.30pm. Downstairs lunch and LO 10pm Mon-Sat.   **INX**

191
xC4

✓ **LUCA'S:** 446 0233. 16 Morningside Rd. '99 leap into town for the ice cream kings to this modern ice-creamerie and caff where kids with dads will enjoy their spag and their sundae. Crowded if not claustrophobic upstairs – they'll love it! 7 days.   **INX**

192
xE1

✓ **GIULIANO'S ON THE SHORE:** 554 5272. 1 Commercial St, by the br. With its checked tablecloths, accented waiters and cheerful pizza/pasta menu, this is almost a cartoon version of an Italian restau – no slight intended – and kids love it. Always a birthday party happening at w/ends. Lunch and LO 10.30/11pm.   **INX**

193
xC1

YE OLDE PEACOCK INN: 552 8707. Newhaven Rd nr Newhaven Harbour and opp Harry Ramsden's (a more obvious place to take kids perhaps, *see below*), but this has been one of Edin's unsung all-round family eateries for yrs, and deserves wider recognition. The fish here really is fresh, the menu is more adventurous than you'd think with lots that wee kids and we kids like. High tea is a treat. Lunch and LO 9.30pm Mon-Thu, 12noon-9.30pm Fri-Sun (till 6pm).   **CHP**

194
C4

FAT SAM'S: 228 3111. 56 Fountainbridge. Cavernous gr Italian-style barn with a couple of enormous television screens, fish tank and animatronic cartoon-like Fat Sam to scare the unwary. The scale and sheer chutzpah appeal to children of all ages (i.e. students' night out). Kids' menu has usual burgers, pizzas and all that jazz. Main menu has all that's jazzier (swordfish, mezzelune) but really a place for the young at heart and brain. 7 days, LO 10.30pm.   **INX**

195
xA3

BRIDGE INN, RATHO: 333 1320. Canal Centre, Ratho, W Lothian. 14km W of centre via A71, turning rt opp Dalmahoy Golf Club. Well worth the drive for an afternoon on, or by, the Union Canal. The Pop Inn Restau has special menus for kids, play areas and numerous distractions. Sailings and walks. LO food 9pm, bar open 12noon-11pm (12midnight Fri-Sat). (307/PUB FOOD) **INX**

196 **CRAMOND BRIG HOTEL:** 339 4350. At the R Almond as you hit Edin on
xA2 the dual carriageway from the Forth Rd Br. This inn has put a lot of effort into attracting families with its indoor/outdoor play areas (Funky Forest). If you've driven for hrs with a whingeing child and want steak and chips while wee Daniel or Amy play themselves into a stupor then it's v convenient. Otherwise a bit characterless. Lunch and LO 9.30pm, 7 days. Open from lunch straight through to close on Sat-Sun. **INX**

197 **HUNTER'S TRYST:** 445 3132. 97 Oxgangs Rd. Adj to Safeway, corner of
xC4 Oxgangs Rd N. Big steaks in the 'burbs. If this place was another half mile S it would be up the Pentlands so a long schlep from town – but nr Fairmilehead exit from bypass, so convenient for travellers. Alloa's bid for kid-friendliness sees a bright Wacky Warehouse play area (it is a warehouse and it's v wacky) connected to pub/inn selling pub/inn food. WW closes 8pm 7 days. Inn till 11pm daily, LO food 10pm (snacks till close).
INX

198 **HARRY RAMSDEN'S:** 551 5566. Newhaven Rd. Edin branch of national
xD1 chain. Bright, tacky, predictable menu, but nice location by harbour nr *Britannia* and the other new big developments. With seats o/side. All day, 7 days. **CHP**

THE BEST TEAROOMS AND COFFEE SHOPS

199
A2
✔ ✔ **GALLERY OF MODERN ART CAFÉ:** Belford Rd. Utterly unbeatable on a fine day when you can sit out on the patio by the grass, with sculptures around, have some wine and a plate of Scottish cheese and oatcakes. Hot dishes are excellent. Coffee and cake whenever. Then it's back to the art. Oh well! Mon-Sat 10am-4.30pm, Sun 2-4.30pm. (359/OTHER ATTRACTIONS)

200
D3
✔ **FRUITMARKET CAFÉ:** 226 1843. 29 Market St. Attached to the Fruitmarket Gallery (397/BEST GALLERIES), a cool spacious place for coffee, cake or a light lunch. Big windows to look out; good mix of tourists, Edin faithfuls and art seekers – the latter go upstairs. Mon-Sat 10.30am-5.30pm, Sun 12noon-5pm.

201
xC4
✔ **MANGO AND STONE:** 229 2987. 165 Bruntsfield Pl. Juice bar in Bruntsfield, the first we suspect of many (in airports, etc.). 'They squeeze to please' and they do, e.g. 'Growing bones' (blueberry, orange, banana, pineapple), the 'Detox' (carrot, orange, beetroot). Filled rolls, good coffee, few chairs. Juice not cheap – health at a premium. 7 days 8am-6pm (Sun 9am-6pm).

202
C2
✔ **QUEEN STREET CAFÉ:** National Portrait Gallery (358/OTHER ATTRAC-TIONS), Queen St, betw Hanover St and St Andrew's Sq. And through the arched window … a civil slice of old Edin gentility. Serving seriously good light meals, tasteful sandwiches, coffee and cake – best scones in town, among other things. Mon-Sat 10am-4.30pm, Sun 2-4.30pm.

203
D3,C4
✔ **FAVORIT:** 220 6880. 20 Teviot Pl, nr Univ, and 30 Leven St, nr King's Theatre (221 1800). First of several branches planned by people who brought us Indigo Yard (320/THESE ARE HIP) and Iguana nearby (326/THESE ARE HIP). Allday, all-round drop-in café in contemporary style reminiscent of City Café (325/THESE ARE HIP). They've thought of everything. Gr late (344/LATE BARS). Both: 7 days, 8am-3am.

204
C2
✔ **THE LAIGH:** 225 1552. 117 Hanover St. Long before the coffee revolution, this basement coffee/bake house was the place to go for café culture. Trad furniture and atmos. Old faves – hazelnut meringue cake, tuna salad – remain despite new owners and are still the best you'll taste anywhere. Ingredients organic where poss. This place is essential Edin. Mon-Sat 8.30am-5pm. Cl Sun.

205 ✓ **WHERE TO?:** 229 6886. 103 Highriggs, Tollcross. Excellent caff/coffee
C3 shop for food, information, inspiration. Report: 230/INTERNET CAFÉS.

206 ✓ **À TABLE:** 220 5335. 4 Howe St. Calling itself a 'continental farmhouse
xD4 café', this is a v Edin New Town experience, incl the one big table for
sitting round à la dinner party. Light, spacious rm and menu. Excellent
sourdough bread is central and all fruit and veg are organic. Sandwiches,
tartines and delicious desserts. Soup and hot dish. Does takeaway and
o/side catering. All stylishly done. 8.30am-5.30pm (10am-6pm Sat). Cl Sun
(but this may change).

207 **CAFÉ FLORENTIN:** 225 6267. 8 St Giles St. Have turned an entire gener-
D3 ation of Edimbourgeois on to almond croissants and wicked tartelettes.
Uptown café with downtown décor, this establishment is the capital in a
nutshell (or shortcrust pastry case). Advocates rub shoulders with student grunge queens over a blast of caffeine. Aficionados feel that
Florentin is not what it was. Discuss (over croissants)! Open 7am-11pm
daily, later during the Festival. Also at 5 NW Circus Pl, Stockbridge – with
shop, 7am-7pm daily. (242/SUN BREAKFAST)

208 **KAFFE POLITIK:** 446 9873. 146-148 Marchmont Rd. All black and white
xD4 and wood and middle-Euro chic at another converted bank in the heart
of student flat land. Rear wall speckled with quotes from assorted celebs.
Damn fine cup of coffee, sodas, juice, soup 'n' sandwiches and unfussy hot
dishes. V good breakfasts available all day Sat and Sun (246/SUN BREAK-
FAST). 10am-10pm daily.

209 **BLACK MEDICINE COFFEE SHOP:** 622 7209. 2 Nicolson St, corner of
D3 Drummond St. Newish coffee shop by the same people as Nicolsons
(92/BEST BISTROS) on busy Southside corner opp Festival Theatre and Univ
Old Quad. Good place to take your book from Thins; get a window seat!
Good smell. Big bagels. 7 days. 8am-8pm.

210 **STARBUCKS:** 226 3610. 128 Princes St, 2nd floor of Waterstone's book-
D2 shop. Dare we say better than the cramped original (Seattle Coffee Co) at
London's Covent Garden? Easily. In among the books, a young and friendly staff dispense everything from caffè latte to iced Americano. Savouries
and pâtisserie courtesy of The Auld Alliance Bakery. View of the Castle.
Open 8am-8pm Mon-Sat (till 7pm Sat) and 10.30am-6pm Sun. Another
more business-like branch in the basement of the Edin Solicitors Property
Centre at 85 George St and a more stand-alone branch in Lothian Rd, on
the corner of Bread St opp the ABC cinema.

211 **CLARINDA'S:** 557 1888. 69 Canongate. Nr the bottom of the Royal Mile nr
E2 the Palace (and the new Parliament building). A small tearoom with hot dishes and snacks that may seem more of a sit-down stop on the tourist trail but
actually has probably the best home-baking in town (esp the apple pie). V
reasonable prices; run by good Edin folk. 10am-4.45pm (from 12noon Sun).

212 **THE ELEPHANT HOUSE:** 220 5355. 21 George IV Br. Nr libraries and Edin
D3 Univ, a rather self-conscious but big-time and well-run coffee shop with
light snacks and multifarious choice of caffeines and tannins to speed
your research. Cakes/pastries are bought in but can be taken out. Mon-Fri
8am-11pm, Sat-Sun 10am-11pm. Same people have **ELEPHANTS &
BAGELS** at Nicolson Sq. Soup 'n' a bagel takeaway and sit-in. 7 days,
8am-6pm (w/ends 10am-5pm).

213 **CAFÉ BARCODE:** 466 8168. 32 Argyle Pl. In the heart of student mort-
xD4 gageland, a new caff contributing to the feel that this street is one of the
coolest and least sussed on the Southside. Good coffee, hot meals and
snacks, and internet access via two Macs (some assistance available).
7 days, Mon-Fri 8am-8pm, Sat-Sun 9am-6pm.

214 **COMMON GROUNDS:** 226 1416. 2-3 N Bank St, top of The Mound. The
D3 kind of coffee emporium where tourists wander in by accident and
women can breast feed with impunity. Cake, light meals, insane range of
espressos, incl the 'Keith Richards' (a quadruple). Live music some nights.
9am-10pm, Sat-Sun 10am-8pm.

215 **G&T (GLASS & THOMPSON):** 557 0909. 2 Dundas St. Patrician New
C2 Town coffee shop and deli with contemporary food and attitude. A
Clarissa Dickson-Wright kind of place: they love food. Gr *antipasti*, salads
and sandwiches to go. 8.30am-6.30pm, Sat till 5.30pm, Sun 11am-4.30pm.
(251/TAKEAWAYS)

216 **BOTANIC GARDENS CAFETERIA:** By 'the House' (where there are reg-
xB1 ular exhibs), within the grds (357/OTHER ATTRACTIONS). For café only, enter
by Arboretum Pl. Recent major revamp but still catering-style food with
light meals at lunchtime. O/side tables; the view of the city is why we
come. And the squirrels. 10am-5pm.

217 **METROPOLE:** 668 4999. 33 Newington Rd. Once a bank, now a civilized
xE4 coffee house – the premises lend an air of Art Deco something. On a quiet
afternoon it's where a Newington mum might mull over her life, the children at the nursery, accompanied by their excellent cappuccino with

cinnamon … and a 'friend'. 9am-10pm daily.

218 **THE LOWER AISLE:** Underneath St Giles Cathedral (362/OTHER ATTRAC-
D3 TIONS), enter round back via Parliament Sq, or through the body o' the kirk.
Proximity of courts sees many legal eagles swooping in, tourists who
have this book and regulars for coffee, tea, light meals. Mon-Fri 9am-
4.30pm, Sun 10am-2pm. Cl Sat.

219 **CAFFE SARDI:** 220 5553. 18-20 Forrest Rd. More a restau perhaps with all
D3 the expected dishes but also serves a mean Danish pastry and espresso.
Coffee machine is a Big Gold Dream and with waitresses from the old
country and Italian television on cable, a hint, just a hint, of Soho's Bar
Italia. Mon-Sat 9.30am-11pm. Cl Sun.

220 **ROUND THE WORLD:** 15 NW Circus Pl, Stockbridge. Exceptional gift
C2 shop and kitchenware vendor with startling coffee bar in converted bank
(once mine). Tea, cake and one of the v best espressos. Open 10am-6pm
Mon-Sat.

221 **LA GRANDE CAFETIÈRE (CAFÉ GRAND):** 228 1188. 182-184
xC4 Bruntsfield Pl. Coffee shop during the day, popular inexp bistro at night.
In among assorted coffees and herbal teas, Bovril can be had. Nice restful
alternative to brash Montpeliers opp. 9am-11pm, till 12midnight Thu-Sat.
Sun 9am-9pm.

222 **CALIFORNIA COFFEE CO:** 228 5001. By the Odeon cinema (Clerk St),
E4, D4 top of Middle Meadow Walk (opp Forrest Rd) and Rose St. 7.45am-9pm
Mon-Fri, 10am-9pm Sat-Sun. Hope Park Cres, 8.30am-7pm Mon-Fri, 10am-
7pm Sat-Sun. Caffeine kiosks in former police boxes. Similar fare to
Starbucks (*see page 58*), but this is on the hoof and home-grown. Others
imminent.

GREAT CAFÉS AND GREASY SPOONS

223
D2

✓ **BLUE MOON CAFÉ:** 557 0911. 36 Broughton St. Longest-established gay café in the capital and still evolving (433/GAY EDIN). Now houses an espresso bar as well as the main bit with breakfast, snacks, meals or a drink. Female staff efficient, boys more spacey. Free condoms in the gents for the impecunious or impatient. 11am-12midnight Mon-Fri, 9am-12.30am Fri-Sat. LO 40 min before close.

224
C4

✓ **NDEBELE:** 221 1141. 59 Home St, Tollcross. The Ndebele are a southern African people, but this café has dishes from all over the continent so get your ostrich, mielie bread and moi moi here – or just have a coffee. Does loads of sandwiches, light meals and has a good groovalong soundtrack. Africa distant and usually hot, this delightfully chilled. Daily 10am-11pm. Takeaway and sit-in.

225
xC4

✓ **LUCA'S:** 446 0233. 16 Morningside Rd. In-town version of legendary ice cream parlour in Musselburgh (486/LOTHIANS). Ice cream and snacks downstairs, more pasta parlour up. Cheap and cheerful food. Gr for kids. 7 days.

226
D1

LOST SOCK DINER: 557 6097. Corner of E London St/Broughton St, adj Sundial laundrette. An innovation and caused a whirl when it opened – a café/restau attached to a laundrette where you could eat well while your washing spun. Several changes of chef and food policy since, still a cool place to snack with or without your powder. 7 days. LO 4pm Mon, 10pm Tue-Sat. Sun 10am-5pm. Same people do the caff at Stills Gallery, Cockburn St (404/BEST GALLERIES).

227
C4

CENTRAL CAFÉ: 228 8550. 42 Home St, next to the Cameo Cinema. Graham Main's downtown deli/takeaway with urban cool and gr snacks and coffee (no cooking). Best music and crack in the area, 9am-6pm. Cl Sun.

228
xD1

CANASTA: 554 5190. 10 Bonnington Rd, nr corner with Gr Jnct St, Leith. Café for locals, not one of your downtown cappuccino numbers. Best omelettes in the burg, and usual café grub (haddock and chips, grills) and cakes home-made before you (I) get up. Tea in a mug. Takeaway. We should honour these people. Cl Sun.

229
E1

VITTORIA: 556 6171. Brunswick St, corner of Leith Walk. An admission: we've been leaving Vittoria out of recent editions of *Scotland The Best!*

How could we? No excuses, let's make amends. Vittoria is one of the best, least pretentious Scottish-Italian scrans in town. Great fry-ups, omelettes and full Italian carbo variants. Sorry! 7 days. 10am-11pm.

KEBAB MAHAL: 667 5214. Nicolson Sq. Cult I. Report: 162/INDIAN RESTAUS.

KUSHI'S: 556 8996. 16 Drummond St. Cult II. Report: 169/INDIAN RESTAUS.

INTERNET CAFÉS

230
C3
✓ **WHERE TO?:** 229 6886. 103 Highriggs, where Laurieston Pl becomes Tollcross. Odd name, odd combo of what are perhaps the preoccupations of proprietor Crawfurd Hill: going out, eating out and IT. Great outdoors lifestyle informs food and décor. Euro food: from rosti to sachertorte and gr fluffy omelettes. Screens incl 2 iMacs (£5 an hr session), but newspapers as well as Internet, so an all-round information destination with good food. A bold and imaginative venture. Then log off – there's hills to climb! 7 days, 7.30am-10pm (10.30 w/ends).

231
C2
CYBERIA: 220 4403. 88 Hanover St. If we can split hairs and say there's a distinction between cool and hip, then Cyberia takes the silicon wafer for coolest capital Internet café. Good coffee, fine sandwiches and cakes – you'd come for an espresso even if you had no interest in cyberspace. 12 terminals, e-mail drop box facility, surfing sessions by the half hr, etc. V chic, understated décor with sculpturey bits. E-mail: edinburgh@cyber-surf.co.uk. Mon-Sat 10am-10pm, Sun 12noon-7pm.

232
C3
WEB 13: 229 8883. 13 Bread St. The city's most homely Internet boutique, 19 terminals. At quieter times, bloke who looks much more attuned to messing around with motherboards will muck in to make you a sandwich. Again, all the usual facs for web, e-mail, etc. Quarter- and half-hr rates, dozen PCs, colour scanning, printing and all that jazz. E-mail: queries@web13.co.uk. The breakfast *sc(ram)bled* egg and mushroom baguette is recommended. Mon-Fri 9am-8pm, Sat 9am-6pm, Sun 11am-5pm.

THE BEST LATE-NIGHT RESTAURANTS

233
C3

✔✔ **BLUE:** 221 1222. Cambridge St. Upstairs in the Traverse Theatre building. The café-bar associated with The Atrium (65/BEST RESTAUS), so the food's pretty good and you can graze and snack till **12midnight** (same menu all day) in the place to be seen (and heard – can be noisy). (79/BEST BISTROS)

234
D3, C4

✔ **FAVORIT:** 220 6880. 20 Teviot Pl and 30 Leven St (221 1800). New, happening café/restau – salads, pasta, wraps, Ben and Jerry's from dawn till almost dawn. More to come. **7 days, 8am-3am.** (203/BEST TEA-ROOMS) **MED**

235
C3

✔ **THE WITCHERY:** 225 5613. Castlehill, top of Royal Mile nr the Castle. Not open v late, but does take bookings up till 11.30pm, that crucial half hr beyond 11 that allows you to eat after the movies. Special after-theatre menu from 10.30pm has 2 courses for under £10, a v good deal from one of the best restaus in town. 7 days, lunch and **LO 11.30pm**. (71/BEST RESTAUS)

236
B2

✔ **PIZZA EXPRESS:** Best branch in Stockbridge 332 7229. 1 Deanhaugh St and W End at 32 Queensferry St (225 8863). **Open till 12midnight** and no booking policy, so a good bet. Report: 118/BEST PIZZA.

237
D2

GIULIANO'S: 556 6590. 18 Union Pl, Leith Walk opp Playhouse. Buzzing Italian tratt day and night. **Handily open till 1am**. Report: 117/ITALIAN RESTAUS.

238
D2

BLUE MOON CAFÉ: 556 2788. 36 Broughton St. Gay café-bar in the quarter. Burgers to bagels. Go on, they won't bite you (or maybe they will). **LO 11.30pm (12.30am Fri-Sat)**. (223/CAFÉS)

239
D3

GORDON'S TRATTORIA: 225 7992. 231 High St. Although some late-night visitors mistake this for a kebab house, it's v definitely Italian. Pasta 'n' pizza until tomorrow. **Sun-Thu 12noon-12midnight, Fri-Sat 12noon-3am.** **INX**

240
D3

BAR ROMA: 226 2977. 39a Queensferry St, nr W End of Princes St. Buzzing day and night. An Edin institution but with recent revamp. Better than your av pasta, smarter than your av wine list. **12noon-12midnight Sun-Thu; 12.45am Fri-Sat.** **INX**

241
A4

PEPE'S TAVERNA: 337 9774. 96 Dalry Rd. Finally, here's one to remember; good and friendly and **open till 2.30am** (though cl Tue). (116/ITALIAN RESTAUS)

242
D3
✓ **CAFÉ FLORENTIN:** St Giles St, off Royal Mile opp Cathedral. The first to open for a civilized start (or finish). The best whirly pastries in town. May be too early to eat cake! **From 7am.** (207/BEST TEAROOMS)

243
C3
✓ **WHERE TO?:** 229 6886. 103 Highriggs, where Laurieston Pl becomes Tollcross. Excellent all-round caff with outdoorsy slant, internet access (230/INTERNET CAFÉS) and good grub. Healthy breakfasts incl Swiss muesli, porridge, kedgeree, bagels, squeezed juice and coffee. Newspapers as well as cyberstuff. **From 7.30am.**

244
D3
FAVORIT: 220 6880. 20 Teviot Pl. The hip all-rounder. **Open 7 days from 8am.** Report: 203/BEST TEAROOMS and 234/LATE-NIGHT RESTAUS.

245
D3
NEGOCIANTS: 45-47 Lothian St. Nr univ. Gr all-round pub (327/THESE ARE HIP), open v late and v early on Sun for breakfast. **From 9am (brunch till 6pm).** May be tables o/side.

246
xD4
KAFFE POLITIK: 446 9873. 146-148 Marchmont Rd. Quite possibly the best scrambled eggs with emmental and chives on toast in town. And good coffee. **From 10am all day.** (208/BEST TEAROOMS)

247
D3
CITY CAFÉ: Blair St. It's been here so long, it's easy to take for granted … but for that 'BIG' breakfast (carnivore or veggie), few places in the city beat the content or American diner atmos. **From 11am.**

248
D2
SMOKE STACK: 556 6032. 53-55 Broughton St. Proper brunch in bar-strewn Broughton St (*see below*) – Arbroath smokies, Eggs Florentine or Benedict, all-out brekkers, vegn or carnivore style in burgundy and blue diner. **12noon-4pm.** (188/BURGERS AND STEAKS)

249
D2, D1
THE BROUGHTON ST BREAKFAST: Meanwhile, elsewhere in Edin's hippest st, the upsurge of café-bar culture offers many good bets for brekkers. From the top down: **THE CATWALK** opens at **10am** for both veggies and carnivores, while **BAROQUE** kicks in from **12.30pm** with similar nosh (slightly more exp). Round the corner in Broughton St Lane, **THE OUTHOUSE** opens at **12.30pm** and serves a more elaborate brunch menu through to 4pm (see THESE ARE HIP for details). For a pubbier experience, try the **BARONY** further down the st (261/GR EDIN PUBS). Cheap, cheerful, papers to peruse. **LOST SOCK DINER** is at the bottom and round the corner. Neighbourhood caff **from 10am** (see 226/CAFÉS).

THE BEST TAKEAWAY PLACES

250
C2
✔ **ROWLAND'S:** 225 3711. 42 Howe St. Still the Top-notch New Town takeaway with creative hot dishes that change daily. Despite the takeaway explosion, still leaves the others standing for real food. Interesting sandwich rolls, excellent cheeses, bread, cakes and now chutneys, oils, etc. Also does o/side catering. Mon-Fri 8am-5pm. Cl Sat-Sun.

251
C2
✔ **G&T (GLASS & THOMPSON):** 557 0909. 2 Dundas St. Deli and coffee shop on main st in New Town, but also takeaway sandwiches/rolls in infinite formats using their drool-making selection of quality ingredients (breads, cheeses, salamis, etc.). Mon-Fri 8.30am-6.30pm, Sat 8.30am-5.30pm, Sun 11am-4.30pm. (215/BEST TEAROOMS)

252
D2
THE GLOBE: 558 3837. 42 Broughton St. A bright spot on the corner in the middle of Edin's coolest st; this place is one of the reasons why. Open all day till 3/4pm for sandwiches/rolls and toasted focaccia. Big window for people watching. Branches at 23 Henderson Row and Castle St. Cl Sun.

253
D2
FOOD PLANTATION: High St. Friendly takeaway with homemade feel (all the baking is fresh and they make the best muffins in town). Sandwiches to go and to order, wraps, crêpes and interesting soups. Odd spot, but definitely worth the detour into the tourist strip. Cl Sun.

254
xA3
THE DELTA: 346 8973. 27 Roseburn Terr. Seriously good Indian takeaway in the W of the city. Good fish and vegn choice. Huge selection, so take away the menu. Some delivery. 7 days, 5-11pm.

255
C1
EASTERN SPICES: 558 3609. 2 Canonmills Br, by the clock. On the grapevine, this place is better than most. Also home delivery. Full Indian menu from pakora to pasanda and vegn meals for one – if you're down at the end of lonely st.

256
C1
HENDERSONS: 556 7737. Canonmills opp the Clock. Takeaway and bakery branch of venerable vegn restau (140/VEGN RESTAUS). Excellent wholemeal meals and sandwiches. Salads, puds, etc. Tables to eat. Other takeaway selection in main shop above restau at 94 Hanover St. Bakery, lunch with LO 5pm. Cl Sun.

À TABLE: 220 5335. 4 Howe St. V New Town takeaway and café (and o/side catering). *Très chic.* Report: 206/BEST TEAROOMS.

VALVONA & CROLLA 'the legendary deli' (page 39)

WHERE TO DRINK

SOME GREAT 'EDINBURGH' PUBS

257
xE1
✓✓ **PORT O' LEITH:** 58 Constitution St. You could walk into this bar once every 5 yrs and be hard pushed to see any changes. Occasionally wild, always interesting; a gr leveller and no place for snobs. The distilled spirit of auld Leith untouched by the new Leith around it. Good soundtrack both verbal and musical. Mary Moriarty is queen of all she surveys. Till 12.45am.

258
D2
✓ **CAFÉ ROYAL:** Behind Burger King at the E end of Princes St, one of Edin's longest celebrated pubs. Unrelated to the London version, though there is a similar Victorian/Baroque elegance. Through the partition is the Oyster Bar (133/SEAFOOD RESTAUS). Central counter and often standing rm only. If you're going out on the tiles, the tiles here are a good place to start. New management, may smarten it up. Mon-Wed 11am-11pm, Thu to 12midnight, Fri-Sat to 1am, Sun 12.30pm-11pm.

259
C4
✓ **BENNET'S:** Leven St, by King's Theatre. Just stand at the back and watch light stream through the stained glass on a sunny day. Same era as Café Royal (*see above*) and similar ambience, mirrors and tiles. Decent food at lunch (296/PUB FOOD). Till 11.30pm Mon-Wed, 12.30am Thu-Sat, 11pm Sun.

260
xE1
✓ **THE POND:** 467 3815. 2 Bath Rd, off Seafield Rd, Leith. V cool Edin bar on the edge of nowhere. They don't make 'em as understated as this and v much on the scene, anywhere else except maybe Amsterdam. Till 1am. (317/THESE ARE HIP).

261
D2
BARONY BAR: 81 Broughton St. Real-ale venue with a young profile and occasional live music; also some Belgian and wheat beers. Newspapers on hand to browse over a Sun afternoon breakfast or a (big) lunchtime pie. Till 12midnight Mon-Thu, 12.30am Fri-Sat, 11pm Sun.

262
D2
THE BASEMENT: 109 Broughton St. Much-imitated, still crucial, this is a chunky, happening sort of, er, basement where you can have Mex-style food during the day served by laaarvely staff in Hawaiian shirts. At night, the punters are well up for it – late, loud and lively. Till 1am daily.

263
xE4
THE SHEEP'S HEID: 656 6952. The Causeway, Duddingston Village. Not central, but a pleasant and dramatic drive away behind Arthur's Seat in the Queen's Park. Old coaching inn with good crack, some locals, patio grd and decent grub (294/PUB FOOD). Food till 9pm, pub 11pm (12midnight Fri-Sat).

264
C2
KAY'S BAR: 39 Jamaica St. The New Town – incl Jamaica St – sometimes gives the impression that it's populated by people who were around in the late 18th century. It's an Edin thing (mainly male). And they care for their beer (285/REAL-ALE PUBS). Till 11.45pm (11pm Sun).

265
B3
MATHER'S: 1 Queensferry St. Edin's W End has a complement of 'smart' bars that cater for people with tight haircuts and powerbooks. The alternative is here – a stand-up space for old-fashioned pubbery, slack coiffure and idle talk (276/'UNSPOILT' PUBS). Till 12midnight Mon-Thu, 1am Fri-Sat, 11pm Sun.

266
E1
ROBBIE'S: Leith Walk, on corner with Iona St. Some bars on Leith Walk are downright scary – but not this one. Tolerant, good range of beer, TV will have the football on often as not. Wild mix of Trainspotters, locals and the odd dodgy character or 3, even a stray social worker (HQ is nearby). Oddly clean after early '99 refurb (274/'UNSPOILT' PUBS). Till 12midnight Mon-Sat, 11pm Sun.

267
D3
CITY CAFÉ: 220 0127. 19 Blair St. Seems ancient, but 11 yrs on, the retro Americana chic has aged gracefully. Pool tables, all-day food, decent coffee. A hip Edin bar that has stood the test of time. Music downstairs later courtesy of guest DJs (247/SUN BREAKFAST). 11am-1am daily.

268
D3
CAFÉ AQUARIUS: 557 6337. 10 Drummond St. Token hip bar in this section for this edition. Swirly lilac pop-tart deco from the makers of Bar Sirius in Leith. Gr soundtrack (guest DJs Fri-Sun evenings), effort goes into the food, eager staff. We are the children of … 11am-1am daily. (324/THESE ARE HIP)

269
D3
THE THREE SISTERS: Cowgate. Of the many booming bars in the Cowgate, we may as well select this one, the latest superbar at the time of going to press and already 'Edinburgh's busiest bar'. Nothing v special but good conversion of old warehouse and better than your av superbar (3 to choose from). Also has rms. 7 days, 11am-1am.

E · 257 260
· 266

1

2

Holyrood Palace

3

Holyrood Park

263 →

4

LONDON ROAD

Calton Hill

LEITH WALK

QUEENS DRIVE

E

THE PLEASANCE

CLERK STREET

NICOLSON STREET

P

· 262

LEITH ST

· 261

YORK PLACE

BROUGHTON STREET

D

· 258

P

NORTH BRIDGE

SOUTH BRIDGE

· 268

· 267

· 269

BLAIR ST

Waverley Station

WAVERLEY BRIDGE

GEORGE IV BRIDGE

COCKBURN STREET

Mus.

University

D

LAURISTON PLACE

PRINCES STREET

HANOVER STREET

DUNDAS STREET

HOWE STREET

ST VINCENT ST

HENDERSON ROW

GLENOGLE ROAD

DUNDAS STREET

HERIOT ROW

INDIA STREET

QUEEN STREET

FREDERICK STREET

CASTLE STREET

· 264

HIGH STREET

GRASSMARKET

Castle

Princes Street Gardens

The Meadows

MELVILLE DRIVE

C

C

MORAY PLACE

CHARLOTTE STREET

· 265

WEST PORT

LOTHIAN ROAD

· 259 ↑

BREAD STREET

Stockbridge

COMELY BANK AVENUE

QUEENSFERRY ROAD

RAEBURN PLACE

QUEENSFERRY STREET

B

QUEENSFERRY ROAD

MORRISON STREET

HAYMARKET TERRACE

Haymarket Station

P

B

DALRY ROAD

1

2

3

4

A

A

THE BEST OLD 'UNSPOILT' PUBS

Of course it's not necessarily the case that when a pub's done up, it's spoiled, or that all old pubs are worth preserving, but some have resisted change and that's part of their appeal. Money and effort are often spent to 'oldify' bars and contrive an atmos. The following places don't have to try.

270
xA4

✓ **THE DIGGERS:** 1 Angle Park Terr. (Officially the Athletic Arms.) Jambo pub *par excellence*, stowed with the Tynecastle faithful before and after games. Still keeps a gr pint of McEwan's 80/-, allegedly the best in Edin. The food is basic pies and stovies. Till 12midnight Mon-Sat, 6pm Sun.

271
xA3

✓ **ROSEBURN BAR:** 1 Roseburn Terr, on main Glas rd out W from Haymarket and one of the nearest pubs to Murrayfield Stadium. Wood and grandeur and red leather, bonny wee snug, fine pint of McEwan's and wall-to-wall rugby of course. Heaving before internationals. Till 11pm Sun-Wed, 12midnight Thu-Sat.

272
C1

✓ **CLARK'S:** 142 Dundas St. A couple of snug snugs, red leather, brewery mirrors and decidedly no frills. Good McEwan's – just the place to pop in if you're tooling downhill from town to Canonmills. A local you would learn to love. Till 11pm (11.30pm Thu-Sat).

273
C3

BLUE BLAZER: 2 Spittal St. No frills, no pretensions, just wooden fixtures and fittings, pies and toasties in this fine S&N-owned howf that usually carries half a dozen real ales. More soul than any of its competitors nearby. Mon-Thu 11am-12midnight, Fri-Sat 11am-12.30am, Sun 12.30pm-11pm.

274
xE1

ROBBIE'S: Leith Walk, on corner with Iona St. Real ales a-go-go in a smoky old neighbourhood howf that tolerates everyone from the wifie in her raincoat to multi-pierced yoof of indeterminate gender. More rough than smooth of course, but with the footy on the box, pint of Bass, packet of Hula Hoops – this bar can save your life (and it's cleaner than it used to be). Till 12midnight Mon-Sat, 11pm Sun. (266/GR EDIN PUBS)

275
C2

OXFORD BAR: 8 Young St, one of the lanes behind W end of George St. No time machine needed – just step in the door to see an Edin that hasn't changed since yon times. Careful what you say; this is an off-duty cop shop. Some real ales but they're beside the point. Till 1am (12midnight Sun).

276
B3, D2

MATHER'S: 1 Queensferry St. Not only a reasonable real-ale pub but almost worth visiting just to look at the ornate fixtures and fittings –

frieze and bar esp. The latter looks as if it was carefully hewn from a sin-gle lump of wood by a Stakhanovite Victorian – they don't make 'em like that these days. Unreconstructed in every sense. Till 12midnight Mon-Thu, 1am Fri-Sat, 11pm Sun. (265/GR EDIN PUBS) There's another, unrelated, **MATHER'S** in Broughton St which is managing to keep its head above water in the city's grooviest thoroughfare by remaining pub-like and unpretentious.

277 **STEWART'S:** 14 Drummond St on the Southside and just off S Br. Lino,
D3 beer, pensioners and folk who sing when in their cups. Few concessions to anything that has happened to the licensed trade since the 1960s. Till 12midnight Mon-Sat, 11pm Sun.

278 **THE ROYAL OAK:** Infirmary St. Tiny upstairs and not much bigger down.
D3 During the day, pensioners sip their pints (couple of real ales) while the cellar opens till 2am.

THE BEST REAL-ALE PUBS

279
C1
✓ **THE CUMBERLAND BAR:** Cumberland St, corner of Dundonald St. After work this New Town bar attracts its share of suits, but later the locals reclaim it and Camra (Campaign for Real Ale) supporters seek it out too. Av of 12 real ales on tap. Nicely appointed, decent pub lunches, unexpected beer grd. Mon-Wed till 11.30pm, Thu-Sat to 12midnight. Sun 12.30-10pm.

280
xC1
✓ **STARBANK INN:** 64 Laverockbank Rd, Newhaven. On the seafront rd W of Newhaven harbour. Usually 9 different ales on offer. Gr place to sit with pint in hand and watch the sun sink over the Forth. The food is good (299/PUB FOOD). Bar till 11pm Sun-Wed, 12midnight Thu-Sat.

281
D3
✓ **THE BOW BAR:** 80 W Bow, halfway down Victoria St. They know how to treat drink in this excellent wee bar. Ask for a whisky – a fair few available – and there's no insane rigmarole about ice in the glass. Laphraoig, for example, comes straight as nature intended. Bliss. Till 11.30pm Mon-Sat, 11pm Sun.

282
D2
✓ **THE GUILDFORD ARMS:** 1 W Register St. Behind Burger King at E end of Princes St (opp Balmoral Hotel) on same block as the Café Royal (258/GR EDIN PUBS). Lofty, ornate Victorian hostelry with loadsa good ales. There are real ales you won't find anywhere else in the city. Pub grub available on 'gallery' floor as well as bar. Sun-Wed till 11pm, Thu-Sat till 12midnight.

283
B3, B1
BERT'S: 29 William St. Rare ales, a suit and twinset crowd after work but a fair mix at other times in this *faux* Edwardian bar. Decent pies for carnivores or veggies alike and a good place to escape from uptown neurosis. Till 11pm Sun-Thu, 12midnight Fri-Sat. More local **BERT'S** at 2 Raeburn Pl, Stockbridge.

284
xC4
THE CANNY MAN: 237 Morningside Rd. Officially known as the Volunteer Arms, but everybody calls it the Canny Man. Good smorrebrod at lunchtime (293/PUB FOOD), and wide range of real ales. Casual visitors may feel that management have an attitude (problem).

285
C2
KAY'S BAR: 39 Jamaica St, off India St in the New Town. Go on an afternoon when gentlemen of a certain age talk politics, history and football over pints of real ale. The bow-tied barman patiently serves. All red and black and vaguely distinguished with a tiny snug – The Library. Till 11.45pm (11pm Sun). (264/GR EDIN PUBS)

286 **CASK AND BARREL:** 115 Broughton St. Wall-to-wall distressed wood, gr
D2 selection of real ales and the only bar in Edin where they've realized that
samosas make ideal snacks. Also does pub grub, sometimes Thai-
flavoured. Till 12.30am Sun-Wed, 1am Thu-Sat.

287 **CLOISTERS:** 26 Brougham St, Tollcross. Nine real ales on tap in this sim-
C4 ple and unfussy bar with its wooden panelling and laid-back app. Same
owners as Bow Bar (*see above*). Basic pub grub at lunchtimes, bar closes
12midnight (12.30am Fri-Sat).

288 **CALEY SAMPLE ROOM:** 5-8 Angle Park Terr. Half-owned by the nearby
A4 (independent) Caledonian Brewery, the CSR sells all the expected
Caledonian real ales and a couple of guests besides. A neighbourhood
bar most of the time, a haven for home and away fans before and after
games at Tynecastle. Basic pub lunches Mon-Fri, drink served till 12mid-
night Sun-Thu, 1am Fri-Sat.

289 **FIRKINS:** Physician & Firkin, 58 Dalkeith Rd; Footlights & Firkin, 7 Spittal
E4, St; Fling & Firkin, 49 Rose St, etc. Coming to us courtesy of Alloa – they
C3, brew their own at Dalkeith Rd and supply all the local Firkins. Formula
C2 pubs – wood, food and real ales from light Summer Swallow to mental
Dogbolter. F*rk*n jokes wearing thin. Generally till 1am daily.

290 **CALEDONIAN BEER FESTIVAL:** An annual event held around the first
A4 w/end in June at Edin's own – and independent – Caledonian Brewery, a
red-brick Victorian pile at 42 Slateford Rd (on rt-hand side going out of
town). It's a gr site, 50 real ales from Adnams to Whitbread on tap, food
and music (esp jazz) on Thu-Sat evenings and Sun afternoon in the brewery's own 'Festival Hall', a refurbed bottling plant. See local press for
details or call 337 1286. The 'Festival Hall' also hosts ceilidhs every Sat.
(428/CEILIDHS)

PUBS WITH GOOD FOOD

291
xE1

✓ **THE SHORE:** 553 5080. 3 The Shore. A bistro/restau but the same (blackboard) menu faster and friendlier in the bar (where you can smoke). Light meat dishes, lots of fish and always something vegn. Lunch and LO 10pm. (89/BEST BISTROS)

292
xE1

✓ **KING'S WARK:** 554 9260. 36 The Shore, on the corner of Bernard St. Woody, candlelit, absolutely fine. A business haunt at lunchtimes and a good informal restau-cum-bar in the evenings. Scottish slant on the menu, incl excellent fish in beer batter and chips; also food at the bar and real ales. Lunch and LO10pm. Bar open to 11pm, 12midnight Fri-Sat.

293
xC4

✓ **THE CANNY MAN:** 447 1484. 237 Morningside Rd (aka The Volunteer Arms) on the A702 via Tollcross, 7km from centre. Idiosyncratic renowned eaterie with a certain hauteur. Carries a complement of malts as long as your arm, serious wine list and excellent smorrebrod lunches (12noon-3pm daily). B-listed building with monkey-jacketed bar staff, cigars for sale – a shrine to the good life. No loonies or undesirables are welcome (you may be tested). Till 12midnight Mon-Sat, 11pm Sun. (284/REAL-ALE PUBS)

294
xE4

THE SHEEP'S HEID: 656 6952. Causeway, Duddingston Village. An 18th-century coaching inn 10km from centre behind Arthur's Seat and reached most easily through the Queen's Park. Restau upstairs (not summer) and decent pub food down, incl alfresco dining when poss. The village and the nearby wildfowl loch should be strolled around if you have time. Food till 9pm, incl Sun.

295
C4

THE GOLF TAVERN: 229 3235. 31 Wright's Houses. Off Bruntsfield Pl facing onto the links. V English country pub style with hearty food (beef 'n' ale pie, sausage and mash), couple of Chesterfields for slumping purposes; clientele can be v MOR. LO food 7.30pm. Bar closes 12midnight daily.

296
C4

BENNET'S: 229 5143. 8 Leven St, next to the King's Theatre. An Edin standby, listed for several reasons (259/GR EDIN PUBS), not least for its honest-to-goodness (and cheap) pub lunch. À la carte (sausage, fish, steak pie, etc.) and daily specials under the enormous mirrors. Lunch only, 12noon-2pm.

297
D2

THE ABBOTSFORD: 225 5276. 3 Rose St. A doughty remnant of Rose St drinking days of yore, and still the best pub lunch nr Princes St. Nothing fancy in the à la carte of grills and mainly meaty entrées. Huge portions. LO in bar 3pm. Restau upstairs serves food in evening too – LO 9.45pm. Bar till 11pm. Cl Sun.

298
C2
THE DOME: 624 8624. 14 George St. Edin's first megabar and not a chain. Former bank and grandiose in the way that only a converted temple to Mammon could be. Main part sits 15m under elegant domed roof with island bar and raised platform at back for determined diners. Staff almost impeccable, pricey menu; you come for the surroundings more than the victuals (MED). Lunch 12noon-6pm, LO dinner 10pm daily. Also snack menu for casual diners away from roped-off posh nosh area. Adj real-ale Art Deco bar Frazers is separate, more intimate, better for a blether. Final bit, downstairs: Why Not?, a nightclub for over-25s still lookin' for lurvv. Main bar Sun-Thu till 11.30pm, Fri-Sat till 1am.

299
xC1
STARBANK INN: 552 4141. 64 Laverockbank Rd, the seafront rd in New Haven. Long-established family pub with real ales (280/REAL-ALE PUBS) and excellent-value food, with big helpings. Gr seafood platter. 7 days lunch and dinner. LO 9pm (Sun all day menu).

300
xD1
OLD CHAIN PIER: 552 1233. 1 Trinity Cres, on the Forth just W of Newhaven Harbour. Rt on the waterfront, off the beaten track. V approachable with friendly staff. Well-kept real ale, gr bar snacks (stilton with oatcakes, interesting toasties) and excellent-value bar meals. LO food 8pm (but ask nicely after 8 and you never know). Bar 12noon-11pm Sun-Wed, till 12midnight Thu-Sat.

301
D4
THE WOK BAR: 667 8594. 30 Rottenrow. More a café/bar restau kind of thing with only table service. Thai/Malaysian/Oriental grub conjured from woks by white people. Hip eaterie in student-land. 7 days lunch and LO 10.30pm (11.30 Sat-Sun).

302
D3
BAR KOHL: 225 6936. 54 George IV Bridge. In this guide once and then forgotten. A reader, John Robb, tells me this is unforgivable: 'It's one of the best bar lunches in this town, never mind the vodka.' He has no vested interest – and who are we to disagree? Only lunch.

OUTSIDE TOWN

Refer to Lothians map on pages 116–117.

303
D1
✓ **THE WATERSIDE, HADDINGTON:** 01620 825674. 28km from town off A1. Longest, landmark pub food watering hole. On riverside, esp ambient in summer. Can feel like England. Upstairs restau and labyrinthine and v publike downstairs. Big helpings. Excellent food. Lunch and supper. LO 10pm.

304 ✓ **DROVER'S INN, EAST LINTON:** 01620 860298. 5 Bridge St. Off the
D1 A1, 35km E of city. Fair way to go for eats, but don't think about the
A1, think about this welcoming pub with notable food. A classic village
pub with warmth and delicious meals in bistro beside bar or restau up
top. Beer grd out back is o/looked and trains whoosh by, but on a sunny
day, partake their excellent lunch here. Lunch and dinner (6-9.30pm)
daily.

305 ✓ **HORSESHOE INN, EDDLESTON nr PEEBLES:** 01721 730225.
xC3 35km SW on A703. Roadside hostelry (has 8rms), but more a restau
than a pub. 7 days, 12noon-3pm and evenings to 9/9.30pm. All day Sun,
incl their estimable roasts.

306 **THE SUN INN, LOTHIANBURN:** 663 2456. On a bend of the A7 nr t/off
C2 for Newtongrange, under mega viaduct, 18km S of city centre. Happy,
homely pub in the unfashionable netherlands of Midlothian. Bistro-style
food, lunch and LO 9.30pm. Always a couple of real ales – one from the
Broughton Brewery.

307 **THE BRIDGE INN/THE POP INN, RATHO, W LOTHIAN:** 333 1320.
B2 16km W of centre via A71, turning rt opp Dalmahoy Golf Club. Large
choice of comforting food in canalside setting. Has won various awards,
incl accolades for its kids' menu. Restau, bar food and canal cruises with
nosh. Pop Inn 12noon-9pm daily. Restau lunch daily and LO 9pm Mon-
Sat. Bar till 11pm, 12midnight Fri-Sat. (195/KID-FRIENDLY)

308 **GOBLIN HA', GIFFORD:** 01620 810244. 35km from town in neat E
D2 Lothian village. One of two hotels, this has the pub grub cornered. Lunch
and supper (6-9pm, 9.30pm Fri-Sat). Grd gets v busy in summer. Nice for
kids.

THE BEST PLACES TO DRINK OUTDOORS

309
C3
THE HUB: 473 2067. Castlehill. The café-bar of the International Festival Centre. Enclosed terr, big brollies, people-watching and decent food. Heater things on chillier days.

310
xE1
THE SHORE: 553 5080. 3 The Shore, Leith. Excellent place to eat (89/BEST BISTROS), some tables just o/side the door, but it's fine to wander over to the dock on the other side of the st and sit with your legs over the edge. Do try not to fall in. From 11am daily.

311
xE1
THE WATERFRONT: 554 7427. 1c Dock Pl. Another v good Leith eaterie (88/BEST BISTROS) but with waterside tables and adj barge for those who fancy a float. Gr wine list. From 12noon Mon-Sat, 12.30pm Sun.

312
D4
PEAR TREE: 667 7533. 38 W Nicolson St. Adj to parts of Edin Univ so real student style with biggest beer grd in the capital and refectory-style food. From 11am Mon-Sat, 12.30pm Sun. Round the corner on the main drag.

313
D3
BAR CE LONA: Round the corner from the above, spills out onto the wide pavement. Food nothing to write home about, but a good mix. (322/THESE ARE HIP)

314
D2
THE OUTHOUSE: 557 6668. 12a Broughton St Lane. Large patio out back, home to summer Sun afternoon barbecues. (Not a gr view unfortunately.) (319/THESE ARE HIP)

315
E3
THE PLEASANCE: In The Pleasance. Open during the Festival only, this is one of the major Fringe venues, and has a large open courtyard. If you're here, you're certainly plugged into the centre of things.

316
D2
THE CATWALK CAFÉ: 478 7770. 2 Picardy Pl. Catwalk café becomes sidewalk café in warm weather. Busy corner on major r/bout, but also the apex of the pink triangle and a traffic light system where traffic stops so maximum people-watching potential. (331/THESE ARE HIP)

General locations: try **GREENSIDE PL**, bars in **THE GRASSMARKET**, and **IGUANA** and **NEGOCIANTS** (326/327/THESE ARE HIP) on **LOTHIAN ST**. All make a stab at pavement café culture when the sun's out.

THESE ARE HIP

317
xE1
THE POND: Corner of Bath Rd and Salamander St, Leith. Turn rt at the foot of Constitution St past the warehouses. This bar is so cool it's on the edge of nowhere. Run by the people who had Edinburgh's landmark easy-listening club Going Places, the Edinburgh Beige Cricket Team and the fanzine, *Shavers Weekly*. This bar is where you'll find the people who know how this town ticks. It's a find and I hope to hell you do – I have a certain interest. Open when you are. (260/GR EDIN PUBS)

318
C2
PO-NA-NA: 226 2224. 43b Frederick St. A case of souk it and see in this popular N African theme bar – part of a chain but not obtrusively. Functions as a bar till 11pm, then it's more of a club with entry charge and DJs, and maybe a queue to get in. 7 days till 3am. The fag machine is covered in zebra skin. Fun, so crowded.

319
D2
THE OUTHOUSE: 557 6668. 12a Broughton St Lane. Not an avowedly gay establishment, but happily mixed of an evening when there's a nice atmos in this v contemporary café-bar. Modish food available 12noon-4pm for self-conscious business diners and a regular Sun barbecue on the patio (not the greatest of views though). One of the few bars in the UK doing the absinthe thing – drink more than 2 at your peril. Till 1am.

320
B3
INDIGO YARD: 220 5603. 7 Charlotte Lane, off Queensferry St. Tucked away in the W End, this spacious designer café-bar offers exposed brickwork, balcony tables, booths and babes in blue of both genders serving good food and drink. More Med than Mex cuisine with flexible menu, but poss too loud later on for serious dining (85/BEST BISTROS). Till 1am daily. Same people have **IGUANA** (*see below*) and **FAVORIT** (203/BEST TEA-ROOMS).

321
D3
OXYGEN: 557 9997. Infirmary St. Latest thang by the people who brought us Baroque in Broughton St and The Water Shed (*see page 81*). The gas to go, along with the usual liquids *à la mode*.

322
D3
BAR CE LONA: 662 8860. 2 W Cross Causeway. Big plate-glass frontage makes fashion statement in student-land. On busy rd for traffic, but often tables o/side. Menu does make attempt at Mediterranea, but mainly a cooler hang out than most on this corner of the Univ. 7 days, all day till 1am.

323
D3
BARACOA: 225 5846. 7 Victoria St. Cuban-style, Cuba Norte (160/MEXICAN RESTAU) may be preferable and more laid back, but 90s UK-Style this

Cuban café-bar prob sets the pace. There is a proper menu till 9pm and wrap snacks after, but it's for the Havana Club and rhythm, this younger crowd come. Ché would think this was only about money – and he'd be right! 7 days all day till 3am.

324 **CAFÉ AQUARIUS:** 557 6337. 10 Drummond St. Pre-club bar spitting dis-
D3 tance from Cowgate venues if you know how to dodge down a close. Guest DJs from Tribal Funktion, Manga, and elsewhere spin tunes. Good chips as well. 11am-11pm daily.

325 **TRAVERSE THEATRE BAR:** Downstairs at the Traverse Theatre,
C3 Cambridge St (410/NIGHTLIFE). One of the first Edin bars to go in for designer furniture, rolling art exhibs and all that jazz. Still trendy if a bit arch. Food 10am-8pm if no show, till 10pm when there's something on. Gr buzz pre- and post-performance. Bar till 12midnight Sun, Tue, Wed; 11pm Mon; 1am Fri-Sat. Much later during Festival when it's one of the nerve centres and around Hogmanay. Good place to meet nice people.

326 **IGUANA:** 220 4288. 41 Lothian St. From the makers of Indigo Yard (*see*
D3 *above*) comes this self-consciously clubby café-bar over the road from Edin Univ's Bristo Sq buildings – so v studenty in term time. DJs (Thu-Sat) play ambient/dub/dance later on. During the day people eat, drink or sip coffee in calm, cool surroundings (by Glasgow's Graven Images). LO food 8.30pm. 9am-1am daily.

327 **NEGOCIANTS:** 225 6313. 45-47 Lothian St. (Pron 'Nigoshunts' by locals.)
D3 Mirrors, food, space and shooters (non-lethal variety) upstairs; dancefloor, DJs (every night), drink and more drink down. Range of clients from civilized bagel-nibblers mid-morning to Chimayed-out dance fiends in the wee small hrs. Zanier and less pretentious than Iguana next door – but just as studenty. Table service lacks pace – but hey! LO food 2.30am. Open 9am-3am daily. (337/LIVE MUSIC)

328 **SIRIUS:** 555 3344. 7-10 Dock Pl, Leith. 'Designed' without being dreadful
xE1 – quite harmonious really and almost democratic in the clientele mix it attracts. Gr energy about the place on the night-out nights, cocktail pitchers abound – wet Wed afternoon muzak would be Massive Attack. Does coffee and food in that eclectic, flexible style (i.e. Med-Mex). Till 12midnight Sun-Wed, 1am Thu-Sat.

329 **THE WATER SHED:** 220 3774. 44 St Stephen St. Neighbourhood café-bar
C1 with *de rigueur* light wood, blue and orange décor. Coffee/food served

10am-7pm (yes, Med-Mex inevitably), really kicks in as a bar later on – open till 1am daily. Share a cocktail or some cheap Chardonnay with Stockbridge's shiny happy people.

330
D3
CITY CAFÉ: 220 0127. 19 Blair St. A true original that went from *the* hippest, to nowhere, and now back again with the cool night people. Buzzing at the w/end, downstairs the DJs play all kinds depending on the night. Good pre-club vibe. Watch the flyers. 11am-11pm daily.

331
D2
THE CATWALK CAFÉ: 478 7770. 2 Picardy Pl. Opened as the bright new thing (concrete grey) in autumn '97 then seemed to go through an identity crisis in '98. Still a cool space for the be-seen crowd though, with DJs in the basement, open decks, etc. And food. Till 1am daily. Tables o/side on a corner of the pink triangle. (316/DRINK OUTDOORS)

GOOD LIVE MUSIC

332
D2
THE VENUE: 557 3073. Calton Rd, behind Waverley Stn. Edin's major live venue at club level with well-established dance clubs at w/ends like Pure and Tribal Funktion. For live music, it's on the UK club circuit, so often notable bands and the best of the Scottish wannabes. Watch for posters and flyers. (424/NIGHTLIFE)

333
D3
LA BELLE ANGELE: 225 2774. 11 Hasties Close. Combines its role as a DJ club and live music venue well. Rm has attitude and atmos. Some show-cases, parties and special nights. (424/NIGHTLIFE)

334
C3
THE CAS ROCK: 229 4341. 104 W Port. Nr art college. Musical oasis in Edin's pubic triangle, the area full of bars with 'dancers'. No-nonsense, Indie/alternative thrashing in small space. Hot, sweaty, beery rock 'n' roll. Till 1am daily.

335
D3
THE LIQUID ROOM: 225 2564. At the top of Victoria St. Probably the city's best turned-out venue for live music. Enter at st level and descend to watch bands before they go on to greater things (or not). For details consult *The List*. Times vary. Also a major club venue.

336
D3, C3
SUBWAY: 225 6766. Cowgate, under George IV Br. Cavernous grungey rock 'n' roll. Fairly studenty, live music some nights, DJs on others playing 1960s to cheesy dance. 5pm-3am daily. Also **SUBWAY WEST END**, 23 Lothian Rd. Glitzier than its Cowgate cousin. Nothing live; DJs playing Indie, 1970s, 1980s.

337
D3
NEGOCIANTS: 225 6313. 45 Lothian St. Basement DJs in bar for young dudes. Upstairs café-bar serving interesting food; bustling with studen-tish crowd, LO food 2.30am. 9am-3am daily. **IGUANA** next door also does cool tunes. Reports: 327/326/THESE ARE HIP.

338
B3
HENRY'S CELLAR BAR: 538 7385. Morrison St. Has established itself as an alternative jazz venue over the last couple of years with sounds of every stripe taking the tiny floor of this crowded basement. Everything from drum 'n' bass experiments to Latin, nightly. Older, mellow crowd. Till 3am.

THE BEST LATE BARS

339 **NEGOCIANTS:** 45 Lothian St, by Univ Union buildings. Civilized
D3 café/restau/bar upstairs and basement with DJs. Open till 3am every
night. Full reports: 327/THESE ARE HIP, 337/LIVE MUSIC.

340 **PO-NA-NA:** 43b Frederick St. More of a club than a bar later on perhaps
C2 but open till 3am daily. Think Morocco. Young crowd; queue at w/ends.
(318/THESE ARE HIP)

341 **THE THREE SISTERS:** Cowgate. 3 themed bars, o/side courtyard and a
D3 'hotel' ensure that this converted warehouse complex goes like a fair –
full 3am, 7 nights. (269/GR EDIN PUBS)

342 **BARACOA:** 7 Victoria St. Cuban nitespot, some food, some salsa. Mainly
D3 rum-fuelled furore and jamming till 3am, 7 nights. (323/THESE ARE HIP)

343 **THE ROYAL OAK:** Infirmary St, nr the top and S Br. Run by ex-White
D3 Heather Club dancer Sandra Adams, this place is a folk institution. Locals
drink in the tiny bar upstairs during the day, and live sessions kick-off
downstairs every night around 10pm with well-kent faces dropping in
occasionally for the tunes and the singaround. Till 2am daily.
(278/'UNSPOILT' PUBS)

344 **FAVORIT:** 19 Teviot Pl, nr Univ. Not so much a bar, but a café/restau
D3 (203/BEST TEAROOMS), but has intentional informal bar atmos, so more 'civilized' than those above if you want more than a pint or a pull. 7 days till
3am.

345 **CC BLOOMS:** Greenside Pl. Late-night gay venue with bar upstairs (catch
D2 the floor show and eye contact generally) and downstairs dance floor. Till
3am. (431/GAY EDIN)

Not-so-very late bars (till 1am) include **IGUANA, INDIGO YARD, THE
WATER SHED** (all THESE ARE HIP).

General area for late bars and ebb and flow of party and night-time ani-
mals is **THE COWGATE – VICTORIA ST – FORREST RD** triangle. Pub hrs
vary, but many places open later than 1am.

IGUANA 'eat, drink or sip coffee in calm, cool surroundings'
(page 80)

WHERE TO GO IN TOWN

Holyrood Palace

↑ 347

• 351

Holyrood Park

QUEEN'S DRIVE

↑ 355

E

LEITH WALK

LONDON ROAD

Calton Hill

THE PLEASANCE

↓ 354

E

NICOLSON STREET

CLERK STREET

P

LEITH ST

P

P

NORTH BRIDGE

SOUTH BRIDGE

BLAIR ST

Waverley Station

BROUGHTON STREET

YORK PLACE

D

348 •

Mus 350

349 •

University

352 •

GEORGE IV BRIDGE

D

HANOVER STREET

DUNDAS STREET

HOWE STREET

FREDERICK ST

HERIOT ROW

CASTLE ST

GEORGE ST

P R I N C E S   S T R E E T

THE MOUND

Princes Street Gardens

Castle

346 •

GRASSMARKET

LAURISTON PLACE

C

HENDERSON ROW

GLENOGLE ROAD

ST VINCENT ST

INDIA STREET

GLOUCESTER LANE

The Meadows

MELVILLE DRIVE

C

LOTHIAN ROAD

WEST PORT

BREAD STREET

Stockbridge

B

RAEBURN PLACE

QUEENSFERRY ST

QUEENSFERRY RD

MORRISON STREET

B

COMELY BANK AVENUE

Haymarket Station

1

QUEENSFERRY ROAD

↓ 356

2

HAYMARKET TERRACE

↓ 353

3

DALRY ROAD

A

4

346
C3
✓✓✓ **EDINBURGH CASTLE:** 225 9846. Go to Princes St and look up. The main attraction, extremely busy AYR. Tartan tea cosies on sale in the shop rake in the bawbees. And yet. St Margaret's 12th-century chapel is simple and beautiful, the rolling history lesson that leads up to the display of Scotland's crown jewels is fascinating; the Stone of Destiny is a big deal to the Scots (though others may not see why). And, ultimately, the Scottish National War Memorial is one of the most genuinely affecting places in the country – a simple, dignified testament to shared pain and loss. Last ticket 45 min before closing. Apr-Sep 9.30am-6pm, Oct-Mar 9.30am-5pm. **HS**

347
E2
✓✓ **PALACE OF HOLYROODHOUSE:** 556 1096. Foot of the Royal Mile. Queenie's N Brit time-share – she's here for a wee while at end June/beginning July every yr. Large parts of the palace are dull (Duke of Hamilton's loo, Queen's wardrobes) so only a dozen or so rms are open, most dating from 17th century but a couple from the earlier 16th-century bit. Lovely cornices abound. Anomalous Stuart features, adj 12th-century abbey ruins quite interesting. Upper-class shop, so get your souvenirs here. Apr-Oct: Mon-Sat 9.30am-5.15pm (last ticket), Sun 9.30am-4.30pm (last ticket). Nov-Mar: 9.30am-3.45pm (last ticket) daily. **HS**

348
C3,
D3,
E3,
E4
✓✓ **THE ROYAL MILE:** The High St, the medieval main thoroughfare of Edin following the trail from the volcanic crag of Castle Rock and connecting the 2 landmarks above. Heaving during the Festival but if on a winter's night you chance by with a frost settling on the cobbles and there's no one around, it's magical. Always interesting with its wynds and closes (Dunbar's Close, Whitehorse Close, the secret grd opp Huntly House), but lots of tacky tartan shops too. See it on a walking tour – there are several esp at night (ghosts/ghouls/witches, etc.). Some of the best actually take you under the st. Mercat Tours (661 4541) are pretty good. Also Robin's (661 0125) and Witchery (225 6745).

349
D3
✓✓ **ROYAL SCOTTISH MUSEUM:** 225 7534. Chambers St. From the big whale skeleton to archaeological artefacts, design exhibs to stuffed elephants, it's all here. Building designed by Captain Francis Fowkes, Royal Engineers, and completed in 1888. Ab fab atrium soars way up high. Mon-Sat 10am-5pm, Sun 12noon-5pm. **ADMN**

350
D3
✓✓ **MUSEUM OF SCOTLAND:** 225 7534. Chambers St. The story of Scotland from geological beginnings to Kirsty Wark's Saab Convertible, all housed in a marvellous new building by Gordon Benson and

Alan Forsyth. Opened in Dec '98, it's even worth paying to get in. World-class space with resonant treasures like St Fillian's Crozier and the Monymusk Reliquary, said to contain bits of St Columba. Mon-Sat 10am-5pm, Sun 12noon-5pm. Open late on Tue and from 4.30-8pm it's free. **ADMN**

351
E3 ✓✓ **DYNAMIC EARTH, THE WILLIAM YOUNGER CENTRE:** 550 7800. Foot of Holyrood Rd. Edin's Millennium Dome, a brand-new interactive museum/visitor attraction, made with Millennium money and a huge success since it opened summer '99. Salisbury Crags rise above, the universe and everything below. Vast restau, o/side an amphitheatre. 7 days 10am-6pm. Winter hrs 10am-5pm. Cl Mon-Tue. **ADMN**

352
C3 ✓✓ **NATIONAL GALLERY** and **ROYAL SCOTTISH ACADEMY:** The Mound. 624 6200 and 225 6671. The National is the rear of the 2 Neoclassical buildings on Princes St and houses a superb collection of Old Masters in a series of hushed salons. Many are world famous, but you don't emerge goggle-eyed as you do from the National in London – more quietly elevated (**FREE**). The Playfair 'temple' on Princes St itself is the **RSA**; changing exhibs which in early summer and midwinter show work from contemporary Scottish artists (**ADMN**). Both galleries Mon-Sat 10am-5pm, Sun 2-5pm. Major refurb underway 2000.

353
xA3 ✓✓ **EDINBURGH ZOO:** 334 9171. Corstorphine Rd. 4km W of Princes St, buses from Princes St Grds side. Whatever you think of zoos, this one is highly respected and its serious zoology is still fun for kids (organized activities in Jul/Aug). The penguins waddle out at 2pm daily and the melancholy, accusing eyes of the wolves connect with onlookers in a profoundly disconcerting manner. Open AYR. Mon-Sat 9am-6pm, Sun 9.30am-6pm. (463/WHERE TO TAKE KIDS) **ADMN**

354
xE4 ✓ **ROYAL COMMONWEALTH POOL:** 667 7211. Dalkeith Rd. Hugely successful pool complex which includes a 50m main pool, a gym, sauna/steam rm/suntan suites and a jungle of flumes. Goes like a fair, morning to night. Some people find the water overtreated and over noisy, but Edin has many good pools to choose from; this is the one that young folk prefer. Some lane swimming. Mon-Fri 9am-9pm, Sat-Sun 10am-4pm (7pm in summer).

355
xE1 ✓ **BRITANNIA:** Ocean Dr, Leith, in the docks, enter by Commercial St at end of Gr Junction St. Done with ruling the waves, the royal yacht has found a permanent home as a tourist attraction (and prestigious corporate night out). Close up, the Art Deco lines are surprisingly attractive,

while the interior was one of the sets for our best-ever soap opera. Daily 10.30am-6pm (last entry 4.30pm). Bookings 555 5566. **ADMN**

356
xA1
√ √ √ **THE FORTH BRIDGE:** S Queensferry, 20km W of Edin via A90. First turning for S Queensferry from dual carriageway; don't confuse with signs for road br. Or train from Waverley to Dalmeny, and walk 1km. Knocking on now and showing its age, the br was 100 in 1990. But still … Can't see too many private finance initiative wallahs rushing in to do anything of similar scope these days – who would have the vision? An international symbol of Scotland, it should be seen, but go to the N side, S Queensferry's getting v crowded – and I live there, goddamit!

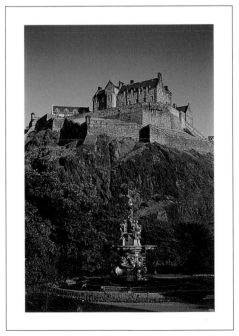

EDINBURGH CASTLE 'the main attraction' (page 87)

357 ✓ ✓ ✓ **ROYAL BOTANIC GARDEN:** 552 7171. Inverleith Row,
C1 3km from Princes St. Bus nos 23, 27. Enter from Inverleith
Row or Arboretum Pl. 70 acres of ornamental grds, trees and walkways; a
joy in every season. Tropical plant houses, the newly landscaped rock and
heath grd and enough space just to wander. Chinese Grd coming on nicely, precocious squirrels everywhere. The 'Botanics' have talks, events (info
552 5339) and other important outstanding gardens throughout
Scotland. Gallery with occasional exhibs and café with outdoor terr for
serene afternoon teas (216/BEST TEAROOMS). Total integrity and the natural high. Open 7 days 9.30am-4pm (Nov-Feb), 6pm (Mar-Apr/Sep-Oct) and
8pm (May-Aug).

358 ✓ ✓ **NATIONAL PORTRAIT GALLERY:** 556 8921. 1 Queen St. Sir
D2 Robert Rowand Anderson's fabulous and custom-built neo-
Gothic pile houses paintings and photos of the good, gr and merely
famous. Danny McGrain hangs out next to the Queen Mum and
Nasmyth's familiar pic of Burns is here. Good venue for photo exhibs,
beautiful atrium with star-flecked ceiling and frieze of (mainly) men in
Scottish history from a Stone-Age chiel to Carlyle. Splendid. Gr café
(202/BEST TEAROOMS). Mon-Sat 10am-5pm, Sun 2-5pm.

359 ✓ **GALLERY OF MODERN ART:** 556 8921. Belford Rd. Betw
xA2 Queensferry Rd and Dean Village (nice to walk through). Best to start
from Palmerston Pl and keep left or see below. Former school with permanent collection from Impressionism to Hockney and the Scottish
painters alongside. An intimate space where you can fall in love (with
paintings). Important temporary exhibs. The café is excellent (199/BEST
TEAROOMS).

360 **THE DEAN GALLERY:** 624 6200. Belford Rd. Across the (busy) rd from
xA2 GOMA. New (1999) addition to Edin art and love life – sexy, intimate spaces,
communal coffee shop, grds to wander. Superb 20th-century collection. Gr
way to app both galleries is by Water of Leith Walkway (365/WALKS IN THE
CITY). Same hrs as GOMA. Mon-Sat 10am-5pm, Sun 2-5pm.

361 **MUSEUM OF CHILDHOOD:** 200 2000. 42 High St. Local authority-run
D3 shrine to the dreamstuff of tender days where you'll find everything from
tin soldiers to Lady Penelope on video. Full of adults saying, 'I had one of
them!' Child-size mannequins in upper gallery can foment an *Avengers*-
era spookiness if you're up there alone. Mon-Sat 10am-5pm. Cl Sun.
(464/WHERE TO TAKE KIDS)

362
D3
ST GILES CATHEDRAL: Royal Mile. Not a cathedral really, although it was once – the High Kirk of Edin, Church of Scotland central and heart of the city since the 9th century. The building is mainly medieval with Norman fragments and all encased in a Georgian exterior. Lorimer's oddly ornate Thistle chapel and the 'big new organ' are impressive. Simple, austere design and bronze of John Knox set the tone historically. Holy Communion daily and other regular services. Good coffee shop in the crypt (218/BEST TEAROOMS). Summer: Mon-Fri 9am-7pm, Sat 9am-5pm, Sun 1-5pm. Winter: Mon-Sat 9am-5pm, Sun 1-5pm.

363
B2
THE GEORGIAN HOUSE: 225 2160. 7 Charlotte Sq. Built in the 1790s, this town house is full of period furniture and fittings. Not many rms, but the dining-rm and kitchen are drop-dead gorgeous – you want to eat and cook there. Delightful ladies from the National Trust for Scotland answer your queries. Moderator of the General Assembly of the Church of Scotland bides up the stair. Apr-Oct 10am-5pm, Sun 2-5pm. Last admn 4.30pm.   **NTS**

364
xA1
LAURISTON CASTLE: 336 2060. 2 Cramond Rd S. 9km W of centre by A90, turning rt for Cramond. Elegant architecture and gracious living from Edwardian times. A largely Jacobean tower house set in tranquil grounds o/looking the Forth. The liveability of the house and the preoccupations of the Reid family make you wish you could poke around for yourself, but there are valuable and exquisite decorative pieces and furniture and it's guided tours only. You could always continue to Cramond for the air (362/WALKS IN THE CITY). Apr-Oct 11am-5pm (cl lunch, cl Fri); Nov-Mar 2-4pm, w/ends only.   **ADMN**

BUTTERFLY FARM, nr DALKEITH: Report: 465/WHERE TO TAKE KIDS.

DEEP SEA WORLD, NORTH QUEENSFERRY: Report: 466/WHERE TO TAKE KIDS.

SCOTT MONUMENT/CALTON HILL: Report: 371/369/BEST VIEWS.

See page 9 for walk codes.

365
A2,
B2,
B1,
C1,
D1

✓✓ **WATER OF LEITH:** The indefatigable wee river that runs from the Pentlands through the city and into the docks at Leith can be walked for most of its length, though obviously not by any circular route. (A) The longest section from Balerno 12km o/side the city, through Colinton Dell to the Tickled Trout pub car park on Lanark Rd (4km from city centre). The 'Dell' itself is a popular glen walk (1-2km). All in all a superb urban walk.

START: A70 to Currie, Juniper Green, Balerno; park by High School. (B) Dean Village to Stockbridge: enter through a marked gate opp Hilton Hotel on Belford Rd (combine with a visit to the art galleries)(359/ 360/OTHER ATTRACTIONS). (C) Warriston, through the spooky old graveyard, to The Shore in Leith (plenty of pubs to repair to). Enter by going to the end of the cul-de-sac at Warriston Cres in Canonmills; climb up the bank and turn left. Most of the Water of Leith Walkway (A, B and C) is cinder track. **12KM (OR LESS) XCIRC BIKE BUS 43,44 1-A-1**

366
xE3

✓✓ **ARTHUR'S SEAT:** Of many walks, a good circular one taking in the wilder bits, the lochs and gr views (370/BEST VIEWS) starts from St Margaret's Loch at the far end of the park from Holyrood Palace. Leaving the car park, skirt the loch and head for the ruined chapel. Pass it on your rt and, after 250m in a dry valley, the buttress of the main summit rears above you on the rt. Keeping it to the rt, ascend over a saddle joining the main route from Dunsapie Loch which appears below on the left. Crow Hill is the other peak crowned by a triangular cairn – both can be slippery when wet. From Arthur's Seat head for and traverse the long steep incline of Salisbury Crags. Paths parallel to the edge lead back to the chapel. (Incidentally, nae mt bikes off tarmac or the polis will have words.)

START: Enter park at palace at foot of the High St and turn left on main road for 1km; the loch is on the rt.

PARK: There are car parks beside the loch and in front of the palace (paths start here too, across the rd).
5-8KM CIRC MT BIKE (RESTRICTED ACCESS) 2-B-2

367
xA1

CRAMOND: This is the charming village (not the suburb) on the Forth at the mouth of the Almond with a variety of gr walks. (A) To the rt along the 'prom'; the trad seaside stroll. (B) Across the causeway at low tide to

Cramond Island (1km). Best to follow the tide out; this allows 4 hrs (tides are posted). People have been known to stay the night in summer, but this is discouraged. (C) Cross the mouth of the Almond in the tiny passenger boat which comes on demand (summer 9am-7pm, winter 10am-4pm) then follow coastal path to Dalmeny House which is open to the public in the afternoons (May-Sep, Sun-Thu); or walk all the way to S Queensferry (8km). (D) Past the boathouse and up the R Almond Heritage Trail which goes eventually to the Cramond Brig Hotel on the A90 and thence to the old airport (3-8km). Though it goes through suburbs and seems to be on the flight path of the London shuttle, the Almond is a real river with a charm and ecosystem of its own. The Cramond Bistro (312 6555) on the riverside is not a bad wee bistro and awaits your return. BYOB. Cl Mon.

START: Leave centre by Queensferry Rd (A90), then rt following signs for Cramond. Cramond Rd N leads to Cramond Glebe Rd; go to end.

PARK: Large car park off Cramond Glebe Rd to rt. Walk 100m to sea.

1/3/8KM XCIRC BIKE BUS 41 1-A-1

363
xA2

CORSTORPHINE HILL: W of centre, a knobbly hilly area of birch, beech and oak, criss-crossed by trails. A perfect place for the contemplation of life's little mysteries and mistakes. Or walking the dog. It has a radio mast, a ruined tower, a boundary with the wild plains of Africa (at the zoo) and a vast redundant nuclear shelter that nobody's supposed to know about. See how many you can spot. If it had a tearoom in an old pavilion, it would be perfect.

START: Leave centre by Queensferry Rd and 8km out turn left at lights, signed Clermiston. The hill is on your left for the next 2km.

PARK: Park where safe, on or nr this rd (Clermiston Rd).

1-7KM CIRC XBIKE BUS 26, 85 1-A-1

369
E2 ✓ ✓ **CALTON HILL:** Gr view of the city easily gained by walking up from E end of Princes St by Waterloo Pl, to the end of the buildings and then up stairs on the left. The City Observatory and the Greek-style folly lend an elegant backdrop to a panorama (unfolding as you walk round) where the view up Princes St and the sweep of the Forth estuary are particularly fine. At night, the city twinkles. Popular cruising area for gays – but can be dangerous. Destination of the Torchlight Procession (part of Edin Hogmanay celebrations) with gr firework finale.

370
xE3 ✓ ✓ **ARTHUR'S SEAT:** W of city centre. Best app through Queen's Park from foot of Canongate by Holyrood Palace. The igneous core of an extinct volcano with the precipitous sill of Salisbury Crags presiding over the city and offering fine views for the fit. Top is 251m; on a clear day you can see 100km. Surprisingly wild considering proximity to city. (366/WALKS IN THE CITY)

371
D2 **SCOTT MONUMENT:** Princes St. Design inspiration for Thunderbird 3. This 1844 Gothic memorial to one of Scotland's best-kent literary sons rises 61.5m above the main drag and provides scope for the vertiginous to come to terms with their affliction. 287 steps mean it's no cakewalk; narrow stairwells weed out claustrophobics too. Those who make it to the top are rewarded with fine views. Underneath, a statue of the mournful Sir Walter gazes across at Jenners. Apr-Sep 9am-6pm; Oct-Mar 9am-3pm. Cl Sun. **ADMN**

372
C3 **CAMERA OBSCURA:** Castlehill, Royal Mile. At v top of st nr castle entrance, a tourist attraction that, surprisingly, has been there for over a century. You ascend through a shop, photography exhibs and holograms to the viewing area where a continuous stream of small groups are shown the effect of the giant revolving periscope thingie. All Edin life is visible – amazing how much fun can be had from a pin-hole camera with a focal length of 8.6m. Apr-Oct 9.30am-6pm, sometimes later. Nov-Mar 10am-5pm. **ADMN**

373
LOTHIANS
D1 **NORTH BERWICK LAW:** The conical volcanic hill, a beacon in the E Lothian landscape. **TRAPRAIN LAW** nearby is higher, tends to be frequented by rock-climbers, but has major prehistoric hillfort citadel of the Goddodin and a definite aura. **BOTH 1-A-1**

THE PENTLANDS/HERMITAGE: Reports: 447/448/WALKS O/SIDE CITY.

CASTLE RAMPARTS: Report: 346/MAIN ATTRACTIONS.

THE BEST SPORTS FACILITIES

SWIMMING AND INDOOR SPORTS CENTRES

374
xE4,
xD4,
xE1,
C1
ROYAL COMMONWEALTH POOL: 667 7211. Dalkeith Rd (354/MAIN ATTRACTIONS). The biggest, but Edin has many others. Recommended are **WARRENDER** (447 0052), Thirlstane Rd 500m beyond the Meadows S of centre; **LEITH VICTORIA** (555 4728), in Jnct Pl off the main st in Leith, now refurbed with Pulse centre; **GLENOGLE** (343 6376) in Stockbridge, the New Town choice, v friendly. All these pools are old and tiled, 25yd long, seldom crowded and excellent for lane swimming – at certain times. All tend to have different sessions, so phone to check.

375
xE1
PORTOBELLO: Portobello Esplanade (461/BEACHES). Similar to others. Recently refurbed, excellent Turkish baths still there, ladies-only, gents-only and mixed days. Phone for details 0131 669 6888.

376
xC1,
xE1
AINSLIE PARK: 551 2400. Pilton Dr, off Ferry Rd, N of centre, 5km from Princes St; and **LEITH WATERWORLD:** 555 6000. Foot of Leith Walk. Leisure centres with water thrills for kids. Ainslie has serious keep-fit side, Leith has financial troubles and opens 10am-5pm Fri-Sun, restricted otherwise.

377
xD1
THE NEXT GENERATION: 554 5000. Newhaven Harbour. V much part of the regeneration of the waterfront, this sportsarama complex in the David Lloyd stable, in fact son of, hence naff name. Terms, gym, 2 pools incl one outdoor o/looking Forth (only in non-wet weather). Not cheap, but not as exp as some in town. 7 days till 11.30pm.

378
xE2
MEADOWBANK: 661 5351. London Rd. City athletics stadium with courts for squash and badminton (often booked), Pulse centre, weights room, 13m indoor climbing wall, outdoor football/hockey pitches and velodrome. No pool.

379
B3
MARCO'S: 228 2141. 51 Grove St. Labyrinthine commercial centre with aerobic classes, gym, squash and snooker. No pool. Little Marco's will look after your kids while you sweat.

380
E3
UNIVERSITY GYM: 650 2585. The Pleasance. No-nonsense complex, v cheap. The best in town for weights (all the right machinery) and circuit training. Squash, badminton, indoor tennis, etc. Quiet in vacs, membership not required. For a reasonable fee, the Fitness and Sports Injury Centre (FASIC) is an excellent alternative to the 'take 2 aspirin and go away' school of GP. Few fake suntans.

381 **EDINBURGH CLUB:** 556 8845. 2 Hillside Cres. Probably the most civilized
E1 of non-hotel-type clubs. Usually members only, longer-stay visitors may
be able to negotiate a rate. Good weights (mainly Universal),
sauna/steam/sun/bistro. Good aerobics classes. And spinning, apparently. No pool.

382 **DRUMSHEUGH BATHS CLUB:** 225 2200. 5 Belford Rd, W End. Private
B2 swimming club in elegant building above Dean Village that costs a fortune to join and has an 18-month waiting list (so nae chance readers). But
gorgeous Victorian pool with rings and trapeze over the water, sauna,
multigym and bar. Frequented by the quality. If you're chums with a New
Town lawyer, get him to sign you in as a guest.

GOLF COURSES

*There are several municipal courses (see phone directory under City of Edin
Council) and nearby, esp down the coast, some famous names that aren't
open to non-members. Refer to Lothians map on pages 116–117.*

383 **BRAID HILLS:** 447 6666. Braid Hills app. 2 18-hole courses (no. 2 summer
C1 only). Thought to be the best in town. Never boring; exhilarating views.
Booking usually not essential, except w/ends. Women welcome (and that
ain't true everywhere round here).

384 **GULLANE NO. 1:** 01620 842255. The best of 3 courses around this pret-
D1 ty, twee village (35km down the coast) that was built for golf. Now you are
really golfing (though not on Sat)!

385 **GLEN GOLF CLUB (aka NORTH BERWICK EAST):** 01620 895288.
D1 Some say W is best (01620 892135) but most say E and few would argue
that N Berwick on a fair day is worth the drive (36km, A1 then A198) from
Edin. That's the Bass Rock out there, and Fidra. Open to women.

386 **MUSSELBURGH:** 01875 801139. The original home of golf (really: golf
C1 recorded here in 1672), but this local authority-run 9-hole links is not
exactly top turf and is enclosed by Musselburgh Racecourse. Nostalgia
still appeals though. **ROYAL MUSSELBURGH** nearby compensates. It
dates to 1774, the fifth-oldest in Scotland. Busy early mornings and Fri
afternoons.

387
D2
GIFFORD: 01620 810267. Dinky inland course on the edge of a dinky village, bypassed by the queue for the big E Lothian courses and a guarded secret among the regulars. (Can't play after 4pm Tue/Wed/Sat or Sun afternoons.) 9 and 11 holes.

OTHER ACTIVITIES

388
xD4
TENNIS: There are lots of private clubs though only the **GRANGE** (332 2148) has lawn tennis and you won't get on there easily. There are places you can slip on (best not to talk about that), but the municipal centres (Edin residents/longer-stay visitors should get a Leisure Access card [661 5351] allowing advance reservation) are:

389
xA4
SAUGHTON: 444 0422. Stevenson Dr. 8km W of city centre. 2 astroturf courts and one other. Also used for football, so phone to book.

390
xC4
CRAIGLOCKHART: 444 1969. Colinton Rd. 8km SW of centre via Morningside and Colinton Rd. 6 indoor courts, 7 outdoor and a 'centre court' – best to check/book by phone. Other separate sports facs incl squash, badminton and gym, 443 0101. Centre open Mon-Fri 9am-11pm, Sat-Sun 9am-10.30pm.

391
xC4
SKIING: Artificial slopes at **HILLEND** on A702, 10km S of centre. 445 4433. Excellent fac with various runs. The matting can be bloody rough when you fall and the chairlift is a bit of a dread for beginners, but once you can ski here, St Anton is all yours. Tuition every evening (not Thu) and w/ends. Open till 10pm in winter, 9pm in summer. Snowboarders welcome but it ain't Whistler.

392
xE4
PONY-TREKKING: LASSWADE RIDING SCHOOL: 663 7676. Lasswade exit from city bypass then A768, rt to Loanhead 1km and left to end of Kevock Rd. Full hacking and trekking facs and courses for all standards and ages.

393
xA4
PENTLAND HILLS TREKKING CENTRE: 01968 661095. At Carlops on A702 (25km from town) has sturdy, steady Icelandic horses who will bear you good-naturedly into the hills. Exhilarating. Bus from St Andrew's Sq.

394
xA3
ICE-SKATING: MURRAYFIELD ICERINK: 337 6933. Riversdale Cres, just off main Glas Rd nr zoo. Cheap, cheerful and chilly. It has been here forever and feels like a gr 1950s B movie … go round! Sessions daily from 2.30pm. Also … **WINTER WONDERLAND:** E Princes St Gardens. Big

open-air ice rink in the gardens below the Scott Monument. Open late Nov-early Jan. 7 days. Mass fun!

395   **ALIEN ROCK:** 552 7211. Old St Andrew's Church, Pier Pl, Newhaven.
xD1   Indoor rock climbing in a converted kirk. Laid back atmos, bouldering rm and interesting 12m walls of various gnarliness to scoot up. Daily; phone for sessions. Have a pint after in **THE STARBANK** or **THE OLD CHAIN PIER** nearby (299/300/PUB FOOD).

THE BEST GALLERIES

396   **CITY ART CENTRE:** 529 3993. Market St. Quite big. This is the place the
D3   populist blockbuster exhibs come to as well as excellent social/education-al displays. Sensibly curated city asset. Convenient and carefully run café.

397   **THE FRUITMARKET GALLERY:** Across the rd in Market St, a smaller,
D3   more warehousey space for more contemporary collections, retrospec-tives, installations. Café (200/BEST TEAROOMS) highly recommended for meeting and eating, watching the world go by.

398   **THE COLLECTIVE GALLERY:** 220 1260. 22 Cockburn St. Installations of
D3   Scottish and other young contemporary trailblazers. Members' work won't break the bank.

399   **INGLEBY GALLERY:** 556 4441. 6 Calton Terr. Important, chic gallery in a
E2   private house backing onto Calton Hill. Often shows work by significant contemporary artists. 10am-6pm Wed-Sat.

400   **THE SCOTTISH GALLERY:** 558 1200. 16 Dundas St. Guy Peploe's influ-
C2   ential New Town gallery on 2 floors. Where to go to buy something paint-ed, sculpted, thrown or crafted by up-and-comers or established names – everything from affordable jewellery to original Joan Eardleys at £10k plus. Or just look.

401   **OPEN EYE GALLERY:** 557 1020. 75-79 Cumberland St and **EYE-2** opp.
C1   Excellent small galleries in residential part of New Town. Always worth checking out for accessible contemporary painting and ceramics. Almost too accessible (take cheque book).

402   **THE PRINTMAKERS' WORKSHOP AND GALLERY:** 557 2479. 23 Union
D1   St, off Leith Walk nr London Rd r/bout. Workshops that you can look over.

Exhibs of work by contemporary printmakers and shop where prints from many of the notable names in Scotland are on sale at reasonable prices. Bit of a treasure.

403 **BELLVUE GALLERY:** 557 1663. 4 Bellvue Cres. Edin's newest small
D1 gallery at the bottom of fashionable Broughton St. Selected contemporary work in light salons (gallery is part of a house). The one to watch, the openings to go to. Afternoons.

404 **PHOTOGRAPHY:** Edin is blessed with 2 contemporary photo-art
D3 venues. **STILLS:** 622 6200, 23 Cockburn St, with a café. **PORTFOLIO:** 220 1911, 43 Candlemaker Row, is a small 2-floor space in what used to be the city's left-wing bookshop.

GOOD NIGHTLIFE

For the current programmes of the places recommended below and all other venues, consult The List *magazine, on sale at most newsagents.*

MOVIES

Multiplex chains apart, these ones take movies seriously:

405 **THE CAMEO:** 228 4141. Home St in Tollcross. 3 screens showing impor-
C4 tant new films and cult classics. Some late movies at w/ends. Good bar.

406 **FILMHOUSE:** 228 2688. Lothian Rd, opp Usher Hall. 3 screens with every-
C3 thing from first-run art-house movies to subtitled obscurities and retrospectives. Home of the annual Film Festival; café-bar (till 11.30pm Sun-Thu, 12.30am Fri-Sat) is a haven from the excesses of Lothian Rd. Open to non-cinephiles.

407 **THE DOMINION:** 447 2660. Newbattle Terr, off Morningside Rd. Friendly,
xC4 family-run cinema with 3 screens (one of them's like sitting in a plane). Nice wee place to see big films with the kids. Luca's ice cream.

THEATRE

408 The main city theatres are **THE FESTIVAL THEATRE:** 529 6000. Nicolson
D3 St. Edin's showcase theatre re-created from the old Empire with a huge glass frontage of bars and a stage and screen dock large enough to

accommodate the world's major companies. Eclectic programme AYR.

409
C4, C3
THE KING'S: 229 1201. Leven St, Tollcross. **THE LYCEUM:** 229 9697. Grindlay St. Ornate and lately refurbed theatres with wide-ranging popular programmes.

410
C3
THE TRAVERSE: 228 1404. Small but influential, dedicated to new work (though mainly touring companies) in modern Euro, v architectural 2-theatre premises in Cambridge St (behind Lyceum). Good rendezvous bar in theatre (325/THESE ARE HIP) plus excellent adj restau (65/BEST RESTAUS) and café-bar (79/BEST BISTROS).

411
C1
THEATRE WORKSHOP: 226 5425. 34 Hamilton Pl. A small neighbourhood theatre in Stockbridge with a wide reputation for vital, innovative work. Café-bar run by the Helios Fountain people (145/VEGN RESTAUS).

COMEDY

Loadsalaughs during the Festival (Fringe), esp at **GILDED BALLOON**, **THE PLEASANCE** and **ASSEMBLY**. AYR at:

412
D2
THE STAND: 558 7272. 5 York Pl. The city's most regular and credible comedy club. Bar and intimate cabaret/club rm. Most nights, always Fri-Sat and full Festival programme.

CLASSICAL MUSIC

413
C3, E4
Usually from one of Scotland's national orchestras at regular concerts in the **USHER HALL** 228 1155. Lothian Rd. Smaller ensembles more occasionally at **THE REID, ST CECILIA'S** or **THE QUEEN'S HALL**. See *The List* or the Sat edition of the *Scotsman* newspaper.

JAZZ

414
E4
THE QUEEN'S HALL: 668 2019. Clerk St. Occasional 'concerts'; see press for details.

415
C3
HENRY'S CELLAR BAR: 538 7385. Morrison St opp cinema nr corner with Lothian Rd. Small, integral jazz cellar (with other funky music). Report: 338/LIVE MUSIC.

416 **NOBLES:** 554 2024. 44a Constitution St. Dependable bar food and real
xE1 ales in a fine-sized rm. Folk on Thu, R&B Fri and jazz Sat, but phone to con-
firm.

417 **LEITH JAZZ FESTIVAL/EDINBURGH JAZZ FESTIVAL:** Late May/early
xE1 Aug. Selected venues. Check *The List* for details or TO.

FOLK

See LIVE MUSIC. *Best bets on a regular basis are:*

418 **SANDY BELL'S aka THE FORREST HILL BAR:** Forrest Hill. Famous and
D3 forever. Sometimes you could look in and wonder why; other times you
know you're in exactly the rt place. Music every night except Tue and Sun.

419 **THE FIDDLER'S ARMS:** Grassmarket. And fiddle they do on Mon nights.
C3 Good crack and blether at all times.

420 **WEST END HOTEL:** 225 3656. Palmerston Pl. A good place to stay or just
B3 to hang out with the Highlanders. Some trad folk live at w/ends and
whenever. (26/INDIVIDUAL HOTELS)

421 **THE ROYAL OAK HALL:** Infirmary St. Late-night singalong. (343/LATE
D3 BARS)

ROCK AND POP

422 **PLAYHOUSE THEATRE:** 0870 6063424. Greenside Pl. Major theatre in
D2 Scotland, most regular programme, holds 3,000. More infrequent as con-
cert venue while they get through the musicals (not many to go).

423 **USHER HALL:** 228 1155. Lothian Rd. Gr auditorium. Classier acts.
C3 Undergoing refurb, so may be absent from current listings.

424 **THE VENUE:** 557 3073 and **LA BELLE ANGELE:** 225 2774. Main small
D3 club venues for emerging and local bands. Check *The List* (fortnightly) for
programmes. (332/333/LIVE MUSIC)

425 **QUEEN'S HALL:** 668 2019. Clerk St. Most diverse (choral, jazz, art pop).
E4 Good atmos. Used every night; your best bet if you just want to go somewhere for decent music.

CEILIDHS

426
C2
THE ASSEMBLY ROOMS: 220 4349. George St. Municipal halls but grand, the venue for all kinds of culture (esp during the Festival), and though a long way from the draughty village hall kind of jig, they've been positively reeling to the sounds of the Robert Fish Band. Ceilidhs generally last Fri of the month. Watch local press, e.g. *The List* (fortnightly), for details and pay at the door.

427
B3
WEST END HOTEL: 225 3656. 35 Palmerston Pl. Edin's Heilan' hame hotel has occasional sessions of music/singing and storytelling (more like a trad ceilidh) but no dancing. This is where to come (or phone) to find out where the others are (occasional ceilidhs held in the church hall nearby). (26/INDIVIDUAL HOTELS)

428
xA4
CALEDONIAN BREWERY: 01698 385251. Slateford Rd. At time of going to press, ceilidhs every Sat in the Festival Hall in the brewery 8-11.45pm. Bands vary but the couple of hundred heuchin' teuchin' punters have a good time regardless. (290/REAL-ALE PUBS)

GAY EDINBURGH THE BEST!

Edin's gay scene continues to develop as the 'pink triangle' around the Playhouse and Broughton St. Gay nights in straight clubs vary – watch flyers and The List, *esp for* **JOY**, **TASTE** *and* **MINGIN'**.

BARS AND CLUBS

429
D2
NEW TOWN BAR: 538 7775. 26 Dublin St. Basement and v sub-basement bar in residential New Town. Mixed crowd. Island bar good for eyes across the rm. Downstairs – called **INTENSE**, open Thu-Sun – is fairly intense; cruisy and gets full-on. That carpet has seen the lot. 7 days till 1am; w/ends 2am.

430
D2
PLANET OUT: 524 0061. Few doors down from the Playhouse by taxi rank (for the dash home) and opp the Deep Sea (for the fish supper if you haven't pulled). Retro poppy look and amiable, mixed crowd. 7 days till 1am. Then you go up the street to …

431
D2
CC BLOOMS: 556 9331. Next to Playhouse. Bar up, disco down. Main event of the evening for most and last port of call for many, so can get *desperate*. Often queues to get in and nr 3am, to get off. After this there's only the 'Gardens of Fun' – more risky than frisky, so get it on here. 7 days till 3am. (345/LATE BARS)

432
E2
STAG AND TURRET: 478 7231. 1 Montrose Terr, Abbeyhill nr well-known cruising area. Neighbourhood local, quietly seedy. 7 days till 1am.

OTHER PLACES

433
D2
BLUE MOON CAFÉ: 556 2788. 36 Broughton St. Friendly and always busy neighbourhood café at the heart of quarter with all-day menu and committed agenda. Non-gay friendly. 2/3 rms with food, drink and conversation. If you are arriving in Edin and don't know anybody, come here first. Food 7 days till 11.15pm, 12.15am w/ends. (223/CAFÉS)

434
E1
NO. 18: 553 3222. 18 Albert Pl. Sauna for gentlemen. Discrete doorway halfway down Leith Walk. Mon-Sat 12noon-10pm. Sun 2-10pm.

435
D1
TOWNHOUSE HEALTH CLUB: 556 6116. 51 E Claremont St, just down from Broughton St. New sauna on 3 floors with bar, open till 11pm. 7 days.

HOTELS

436
D2
MANSFIELD HOUSE: 556 7980. 57 Dublin St. Small New Town guest house and OK gay stay. Candelabra in the hall, various other camperie. Breakfast on a tray. No public rms – you'll have to leave your door open. New Town Bar (*see above*) up the st.

5RMS	**JAN-DEC**	**X/X**	**XPETS**	**XCC**	**XKIDS**	**MED.INX**

437
B3
ST VALERY GH: 337 1893. 36 Coates Gardens, W End. Gay-friendly rather than gay GH by the people who used to have the Linden Hotel.

20RMS	**JAN-DEC**	**T/T**	**XPETS**	**CC**	**KIDS**	**INX**

438
xE1
GARLANDS: 554 4205. 48 Pilrig St. Quiet st of many other guesthouses about 2km from scene (but nr sauna).

6RMS	**JAN-DEC**	**X/T**	**PETS**	**XCC**	**KIDS**	**CHP**

439
xE4
SOUTHSIDE GH: 668 4422. 8 Newington Rd nr Commonwealth Pool. Not too far away and well-appointed GH, mainly gay. No smk.

7RMS	**JAN-DEC**	**X/T**	**XPETS**	**CC**	**KIDS**	**INX**

Edin club culture still getting better. Most clubs are still weekly or occasional events, but they tend to use the same venues. These are the ones to check:

440 **E2K:** 478 7434. 14 Picardy Pl. Major Edin club venue. Same people have
D2 The Outhouse (319/THESE ARE HIP) and good location nr Playhouse and gay zone. 2 floors in former casino. Always Fri-Sat, maybe others (Sun was Queer Sunday at time of going to press).

441 **THE VENUE:** 557 3073. Calton Rd behind Waverley Stn. Long-established
D2 (in club terms) venue for clubs on w/end nights (mainly live bands during the week). Top nights – **PURE** (considered a major club night in Scotland), **TRIBAL FUNKTION, DISCO INFERNO.**

442 **THE BONGO CLUB**: 556 5204. 14 New St. A small door in a big wall above
D2 a huge underground parking lot (formerly the bus garage). Big windows onto small rms where a committed crowd have created a club which is truly underground. No isms here incl ageism. W/ends, but may close some time in 2000.

443 **LA BELLE ANGELE:** 225 2774. Hastie's Close off Cowgate at Gilded
D2 Balloon. W/ends. Occupants vary, we couldn't say (except we love **MANGA**).

444 **CAVENDISH:** 228 3252. W Tollcross, upstairs it has the long-running **THE**
D2 **MAMBO CLUB** Fri and Sat (on 2 floors). African/reggae/generally good vibes music for v mixed crowd – good for oldies who like to dance.

445 **MERCADO:** 226 4224. 36-39 Market St behind Waverley Stn. Probably
D2 Edinburgh's longest-running club venue. Famous Fri night pre-club piss-up and singles thing (5-10pm) and more mid-range and cheesy music clubs like **TIME TUNNEL** and **VIVA**.

446 **THE DOME:** 624 8633. George St. Home to **WHY NOT?** Disco-mating
D2 venue for over-25s. More select than **EROS/ELITE** which you may hear about (at the Fountainpark Leisure Complex – avoid!)

WHERE TO GO OUT OF TOWN

Refer to Lothians map on pages 116–117.

447
B2
✓ **THE PENTLANDS:** A serious range of hills rising to almost 600m, remote in parts and offering some fine walking. There are many paths up the various tops and round the lochs and reservoirs. (A) A good start in town is made by going off the bypass at Colinton, follow signs for Colinton Village, then the left fork up Woodhall Rd. Second left up Bonaly Rd (signed Bonaly Scout Camp). Drive/walk as far as you can (2km) and park by the gate leading to the hill proper where there is a map showing routes. The path to Glencorse is one of the classic Pentland walks. (B) Most walks start from signposted gateways on the A702 Biggar Rd. There are starts at Boghall (5km after Hillend ski slope); on the long straight stretch before Silverburn (a 10km path to Balerno); from Habbie's Howe about 18km from town; and from the village of Carlops, 22km from town. (C) The most popular start is probably from the visitor centre behind the Flotterstone Inn, also on the A702, 14km from town (decent pub lunch and 6-10pm, all day w/ends); trailboard and ranger service. The remoter tops around Loganlea Reservoir are worth the extra mile.

1-20KM CAN BE CIRC MTBIKE BUS 4 OR ST ANDR SQ 2-B-2

448
C2
HERMITAGE OF BRAID: Strictly speaking, still in town, but a real sense of being in a country glen and from the windy tops of the Braid Hills there are some marvellous views back over the city. Main track along the burn is easy to follow and you eventually come to Hermitage House info centre; any paths ascending to the rt take you to the ridge of Blackford Hill. In winter, there's a gr sledging place over the first br up to the left and across the main rd.

START: Blackford Glen Rd. Go S on Mayfield to main T-jnct with Liberton Rd, turn rt (signed Penicuik) then hard rt.

1-4KM CAN BE CIRC XBIKE BUS 7 1-A-1

449
C2
ROSLIN GLEN: Special: spiritual, historical and enchanting, with a chapel, a ruined castle and woodland walks along the R Esk.

START: A701 from Mayfield or Newington (or bypass, t/off Penicuik, A702 then fork left on A703 to Roslin). Some parking at chapel, 500m from corner of Main St/Manse Rd, or follow B7003 to Rosewell (also marked Rosslynlee Hospital) and 1km from village the main car park is to the left. (469/BEST PLACES IN THE LOTHIANS)

1-8KM XCIRC BIKE BUS ST ANDR SQ 1-A-1

450 **ALMONDELL:** A country park to W of city (18km) nr (and one of the best
B2 things about) Livingston. A deep, peaceful woody cleft with easy paths
and riverine meadows. Fine for kids, lovers and dog walkers. Visitor centre
with teashop. Trails marked.

START: Best app from Edin by A71 via Sighthill. After Wilkieston, turn rt
for Camp (B7015) then follow signs. Or A89 to Broxburn past start of M8.
Follow signs from Broxburn.   **2-8KM XCIRC BIKE BUS ST ANDR SQ 1-A-1**

451 **BEECRAIGS and COCKLEROY HILL:** Another country park SW of
B1 Linlithgow with trails and clearings in mixed woods, a deer farm and a
fishing loch. Gr adventure playground for kids. Best is the climb and extraordinary view from Cockleroy Hill, far better than you'd expect for the
effort. From Ben Lomond to the Bass Rock; and the gunge of
Grangemouth in the sky to the E.

START: M90 to Linlithgow (26km), through town and left on Preston Rd.
Go on 4km, park is signed, but for hill you don't need to take the left turn.
The hill, and nearest car park to it, are on the rt.
                        2-8KM CIRC MTBIKE BUS ST ANDR SQ 1-A-1

452 **BORTHWICK and CRICHTON CASTLES:** Takes in 2 impressive castles,
C2 the first a posh hotel (53/HOTELS O/SIDE TOWN) and the other an imposing
ruin on a ridge o/looking the Tyne. A walk through dramatic Border
Country steeped in lore. Path obvious at first in either direction, then
peters out, but the castle you're going to is always in view. Nice picnic
spots nr Crichton. (471/BEST PLACES IN THE LOTHIANS)

START: From Borthwick: A7 S for 16km, past Gorebridge, left at N
Middleton; signed. From Crichton: A68 almost to Pathhead, signed then
3km.   **7KM XCIRC XBIKE BUS ST ANDR SQ 1-B-2**

THE BEST WOODLAND WALKS

Refer to Lothians map on pages 116–117.

453 **DAWYCK GARDENS, nr STOBO:** 10km W of Peebles on B712 Moffat rd.
xD3 Outstn of the Edin Botanics; a 'recent' acquisition, though tree planting here goes back 300 yrs. Sloping grounds around the Scrape Burn which trickles into the Tweed. Landscaped woody pathways for meditative walks. Famous for shrubs and blue Himalayan poppies. Mar-Oct 10am-6pm. ADMN

454 **HUMBIE WOODS:** 25km SE by A68 t/off at Fala. Follow signs for church.
C2 Most open woods (beech) beyond car park, through paddock. The churchyard is as reassuring a place to be buried as you could wish for; if you're set on cremation, come here and think of earth. Deep in the woods with the burn besides; after-hrs the sprites and the spirits must have a hell of a time.

455 **SMEATON GARDENS, EAST LINTON:** 2km from village on N Berwick
D1 rd (signed Smeaton). Up a drive in an old estate is this walled grd going back to the early 19th century. An additional pleasure is the Lake Walk halfway down the drive through a small gate in the woods. A 1km stroll round a secret finger lake in magnificent woodland. Grd hrs 10am-4.30pm, Sun from 11.30am; cl w/ends Jan and Feb.

456 **WOODHALL DENE, nr DUNBAR:** A1 Dunbar bypass, E to Spott then rd
E1 to left, 5km. Small car park in river hollow. Follow river to important ancient woodland site (2km). Can be damp. Few folk.

457 **DALKEITH COUNTRY PARK:** 15km SE by A68. The wooded policies of
C2 Dalkeith House; enter at end of Main St. Surprisingly extensive area so close to town and conurbation. Under these stately deciduous trees, carpets of bluebells, daffs and snowdrops, primroses and wild garlic according to season. Adventure playground for kids, natural playground for the rest of us.

458 **VOGRIE COUNTRY PARK, nr GOREBRIDGE:** 25km S by A7 then B6372
C2 6km from Gorebridge. Small country park well organized for 'recreational pursuits'. 9-hole golf course, tearoom and country ranger staff. May be busy on Sun, but otherwise a corral of countryside on the v edge of town.

459 **CARDRONA FOREST/GLENTRESS, nr PEEBLES:** 40km S to Peebles,
xD3 8km E on B7062 and similar distance on A72. Cardrona on same rd as Kailzie Grd Tearoom (Apr-Oct) is excellent. Forestry Commission woodlands so mostly regimented firs, but Scots pine and deciduous trees up

the burn. Set trails incl mt bikes. Nice in late autumn and winter. Some dark mysterious bits.

MUIRAVONSIDE COUNTRY PARK: Report: 481/BEST PLACES IN THE LOTHIANS.

BEECRAIGS and COCKLEROY HILL: Report: 451/EASY WALKS O/SIDE THE CITY.

THE BEST BEACHES

Refer to Lothians map on pages 116–117.

460
E1

✓ **SEACLIFF:** The best beach, least crowded/littered; perfect for pic-nics, beachcombing, and gazing into rock pools. There is a harbour, still in use, which is also good for swimming. 50km from Edin, Seacliff is off the A198 out of N Berwick, 3km after Tantallon Castle (472/BEST PLACES IN THE LOTHIANS). At a bend in the rd and a farm (Auldhame) there is an unsigned rd off to the left. 2km on there's a barrier, costing 2 x 50p to get car through. Car park 1km then walk. From A1, take E Linton t/off, go through Whitekirk towards N Berwick, then same.

461
C1

PORTOBELLO: Edin's town beach, 8km from centre by London Rd. When sunny – chips, lager, bad ice cream. When miserable – soulful dog walkers. Arcades, mini-funfair, long prom. A 'used to be' place – maybe the *Evening News* will shame the council enough and it will be reinstated to its former glory. (375/SPORTS FACS)

462
D1

YELLOWCRAIGS: Nearest decent beach (35km). A1 or bypass, then A198 coast rd. Left o/side Dirleton for 2km, park and walk 100m across links to fairly clean strand and sea. Gets busy, but big enough to share. Hardly anyone swims, but you can. Scenic. **GULLANE BENTS**, a sweep of beach, is nearby and reached from village main st. Connects westwards with Aberlady Nature Reserve. One of the cleanest.

463
xA3

✓ ✓ **EDINBURGH ZOO:** 334 9171. Corstorphine Rd. 4km W of Princes St. A large and long-established zoo, where the natural world from the poles to the plains of Africa is ranged around Corstorphine Hill. Enough huge/exotic/ghastly creatures and friendly, amusing ones to fill an overstimulated day. The penguins and the seals do their stuff at set times. More familiar creatures hang out at the 'farm'. Café and shop stocked with environmentally OK toys and souvenirs. Open 7 days 9am-6pm (until dusk in winter). (353/MAIN ATTRACTIONS)   **ADMN**

464
D3

✓ ✓ **MUSEUM OF CHILDHOOD:** 529 4142. 42 High St. An Aladdin's cave of toys through and for all ages. Full of adults saying, 'I had one of them!' Much more fascinating than computer games – allegedly. Mon-Sat 10am-5pm. Cl Sun. (361/OTHER ATTRACTIONS)

465
LOTHIANS
C2

✓ **BUTTERFLY FARM, nr DALKEITH:** 663 4932. On A7, signed Eskbank/Galashiels from ring rd (1km). Part of a big complex which includes a grd centre and the revamped and rather swish **BIRDS OF PREY CENTRE** (flying displays; kids get to handle some of the birds, phone for details on 654 1720). As for the bugs, the butterflies are delightful but 'orrible children will be far more impressed with the scorpions, locusts and other assorted uglies on show. Red-kneed tarantula not for the faint-hearted. 7 days, 10am-5pm.

466
LOTHIANS
B1

✓ **DEEP SEA WORLD, NORTH QUEENSFERRY:** 01383 411411. The massively successful aquarium in a quarry which must make life hell in N Queensferry at the w/end (park 'n' ride system and buses from Edin, or better still by *Maid of the Forth* from S Queensferry. Habitats are viewed from a conveyor belt where you can stare goggle-eyed at the goggle-eyed fish teeming around and above you. Poor old Moby the whale's skull is now displayed (he got into trouble in the Forth in 1997) along with Amazonian fish in a 'rainforest habitat'. Maximum hard sell to this all-weather attraction, but kids like it even when they've been queuing for aeons. In my view the best thing is the view from the canteen. Open AYR 7 days: summer 10am-6.30pm; winter 11am-5pm.   **ADMN**

467   **CHILDREN'S FESTIVAL:** 554 6297 for info. Annual event held sometime in May somewhere in the capital, possibly in tents. Yes, there were changes afoot when the book was being written but the kids' fest, a week of shows from around the world, is always good fun.

BEST PLACES IN THE LOTHIANS

Refer to Lothians map on pages 116–117.

HISTORICAL PLACES

468
B1

✓ ✓ ✓ **LINLITHGOW PALACE:** Impressive from the M9 and the S app to this, the most agreeable of W Lothian towns, but don't confuse the magnificent Renaissance edifice with St Michael's Church next door, topped with its controversial crown and spear spire. From the richly carved fountain in the courtyard, to the Gr Hall with its adj huge kitchens, you get a real impression of the lavish lifestyle of the court. Apparently 'underperforms' as an attraction for Historic Scotland, so some titivation may be underway. **HS**

469
C2

✓ ✓ **ROSSLYN CHAPEL:** 12 km S of Edin city centre. Take A702, then A703 from ring-route rd, marked Penicuik. Roslin village 1km from main rd and chapel 500m from village crossrds above Roslin Glen (449/WALKS O/SIDE THE CITY). Freemason central: stories abound of the Holy Grail hidden in the walls and for the next few yrs there's a metal hood to protect the roof. For such a wee chapel visitors can spend hrs wandering around working out the place, with help from copious guidance notes. Founded by a 15th-century Sinclair, Prince of Orkney, who reinterred his 13th-century ancestor here (the latter just happened to be a Grand Prior of the Knights Templar). All holy meaningful stuff in a *Foucault's Pendulum* sense. But a special place. Episcopalian.

470
A1

CAIRNPAPPLE HILL, nr LINLITHGOW: App from the Beecraigs' rd off W end of Linlithgow main st. Go past the Beecraigs t/off and continue for 3km. Cairnpapple is signed. Cairn and remnants of various rings of stones evince the long sequence of ceremonial activities that took place on this high, windy hill betw 2800 and 500 BC. Atmos made even more strange by the very 20th-century communications mast next door. Go into the tomb. **HS**

471
C2

CRICHTON CASTLE, nr PATHHEAD: 6km W of A68 at Pathhead (28km S of Edin) or via A7 turning E 3km S of Gorebridge. Massive Border keep dominating the Tyne valley on knoll with church ruin nearby. Spectacular 'range' built late 16th century. 500m walk from Crichton village. Good picnic spot. (452/WALKS O/SIDE THE CITY) **HS**

472
D1

TANTALLON CASTLE, NORTH BERWICK: 5km E of town by coast rd; 500m to dramatic clifftop setting with views to Bass Rock. Dates from 1350 with massive 'curtain wall' to see it through stormy weather and stormy history. The Red Douglases and their friends kept the world at bay. Gr beach nearby (440/BEACHES).

473 **HOPETOUN MONUMENT, ATHELSTANEFORD, nr HADDINGTON:**
D1 The needle atop a rare rise in E Lothian and a gr vantage point from which to view the county from the Forth to the Lammermuirs and Edin over there. Off A6737 Haddington to Aberlady rd on B1343 to Athelstaneford. Car park and short climb. Tower usually open and viewfinder boards at the top. Good gentle 'ridge' walk E from here.

474 **GOSFORD HOUSE, nr ABERLADY:** On A198 betw Longniddry and
D1 Aberlady, the Gosford estate is behind a high wall and strangely stunted vegetation. Imposing house with centre block by Robert Adam and the wing you visit by William Young. The Marble Hall houses the remarkable collections of the unbroken line of the Earls of Wemyss. Botticellis, Rubens and Canalettos and important portraits in delightful informal displays (handwritten cards). No tearoom or paraphernalia here, but the grounds with their ornamental ponds and their Hansel and Gretel curling and ice houses are superb picnic spots. Only open Wed/Sat/Sun 2-5pm, Jun and Jul.

475 **THE LAMP OF THE LOTHIANS, ST MARY'S COLLEGIATE, HAD-**
D1 **DINGTON:** Follow signs from E main st. At the risk of sounding profane or at least trite, this is a church that's really got its act together, both now and throughout ecclesiastical history. It's beautiful and in a fine setting on the R Tyne, with good stained glass and interesting crypts and corners. But it's obviously v much at the centre of the community, a lamp as it were, in the Lothians. Guided tours, brass rubbings (Sat), summer recitals (Sun afternoon). Coffee shop and gift shop. Don't miss Lady Kitty's grd nearby, incl the secret medicinal grd, a quiet spot to contemplate (if not sort out) your condition. Apr-Sep Mon-Sat 10am-4pm.

476 **EAST LOTHIAN CHURCHES at ABERLADY, WHITEKIRK and**
D1 **ATHELSTANEFORD:** 3 charming churches in bucolic settings; quiet corners to explore and reflect. Easy to find. All have interesting local histories and in the case of Athelstaneford, a national resonance – a 'vision' in the sky nr here became the flag of Scotland, the saltire. An innovative audiovisual display explains. Aberlady my favourite.

OUTDOOR PLACES *Also see* WALKS O/SIDE THE CITY.

477
xE1

✓ ✓ **ST ABB'S HEAD, nr NORTH BERWICK:** Outwith Lothians, 22 km from N Berwick, 9km N of Eyemouth but only 10km E of main A1. Spectacular cliff scenery, a huge seabird colony, rich marine life and a varied flora make this a place of fascination and diverse interest. Good view from top of stacks, geos and cliff face full of serried ranks of guillemot, kittiwake, razorbill, etc. Hanging grds of grasses and campion. Behind cliffs, grassland rolls down to the Mire L and its varied habitat of bird, insect and butterfly life and vegetation. Superb.

478
C1

✓ **THE LAGOON, MUSSELBURGH:** On E end of town behind the racecourse (follow rd round), at the estuarine mouth of the R Esk. Waders, seabirds, ducks aplenty and often interesting migrants on the mudflats and wide littoral. The 'lagoon' itself is a man-made pond behind and attracts big populations (both birds and binocs). This is the nearest diverse-species area to Edin (15km) and in recent yrs has become one of the most significant migrant stopovers in the UK.

479
E2

THE LAMMERMUIRS: The hills SE of Edin that divide the rich farmlands of E Lothian and the valley of the Tweed in the Borders. Mostly a high wide moorland but there's wooded gentle hill country in the watersheds of the southern rivers and spectacular coastal scenery betw Cockburnspath and St Abb's Head. The eastern part of the Southern Upland Way follows the Lammermuirs to the coast. Many moorland walks begin at the car park at the head of Whiteadder Reservoir (A1 to Haddington, B6369 towards Humbie, then E on B6355 through Gifford), a mysterious loch in the bowl of the hills. Excellent walks also centre on Abbey St Bathans to the S. Head off the A1 at Cockburnspath. Through village to 'Toot' Corner (signed 1km) and off to left, follow path above valley of Whiteadder to Edinshall Broch (2km). Further on, along river (1km), is a swing br and a fine place to swim. Circular walk possible; ask in village.

5-15KM SOME CIRC MTBIKE 1/2-B-2

480
E1

JOHN MUIR COUNTRY PARK, nr DUNBAR: Named after the 19th-century conservationist who founded America's National Parks (and the Sierra Club) and who was born in Dunbar. This swathe of coastline to the W of the town (known locally as Tyninghame) is an important estuarine nature reserve but is good for family walks and beachcombing. Can enter via B6370 off A198 to N Berwick or by 'clifftop' trail from Dunbar.

Where to go out of Town

481 **MUIRAVONSIDE COUNTRY PARK:** 5km W of Linlithgow on B825. Also
A1 signposted from jnct 4 of the M9 Edin/Stirling. Former farm estate now
run by the local authority providing 170 acres of woodland walks, park-
land, picnic sites and a visitor centre for school parties or anyone else with
an interest in birds, bees and badgers. Ranger service does guided walks
Apr-Sep. Gr place to walk off that lunch at the none-too-distant
Champany's (183/BURGERS AND STEAKS).

482 **THE BASS ROCK, off NORTH BERWICK:** 'Temple of gannets'. A gr
D1 guano-encrusted spaceship takeoff ramp sticking out of the Forth and
where Davie Balfour was imprisoned in RLS's *Catriona* (aka *Kidnapped* 2).
Weather-dependent boat trips available May-Sep courtesy of Mr Marr
from N Berwick harbour (also to nearby Fidra). Phone 01620 892838 for
details.

ACTIVITY PLACES *Also see* SPORTS FACILITIES.

483 ✔ **LINLITHGOW POOL:** 01506 652783. On edge of pleasant town off
B1 rd to Lanark. Modern light and airy sports centre with sauna and
steam room at the poolside and W Lothian o/side the windows. Excellent
community facility, well designed and laid out. All towns should enjoy this
quality of life. This pool is where I go.

484 ✔ **PORT EDGAR, SOUTH QUEENSFERRY:** 331 3330. At end of vil-
B1 lage, under and beyond the Forth Rd Br. Major marina and water-
sports centre. Berth your boat, hire anthing from a Wayfarer to a canoe or
just use the jetty to kick off some windsurfing or jet-skiing. Big tuition
programme for kids. Easter-Oct..

485 **DUNBAR POOL:** 01368 865456. Model of its kind, o/looking old harbour
E1 (where folks used to swim on a summer's day) and castle ruins. Cool, modern
design amid the warm red sandstone. Flumes and wave machine that mim-
ics the sea o/side; lengths just possible in betw (though it's often v crowded).
7 days until 8pm (6pm at w/ends).

OTHER MUSTS

486 ✔ ✔ **LUCA'S, MUSSELBURGH:** 32 High St. Queues in the middle of
C1 a Sun afternoon in Feb are testament to the enduring populari-
ty of this legendary ice-cream boutique. 3 classic flavours (vanilla, choc
and strawberry) and pure ingredients attract folk from Edin (14km). Café
through the back has basic snacks and ice cream in its sundae best, but

you might have to wait when it gets busy. Mon-Sat 9am-10pm, Sun 10.30am-10pm.

487 ✔ ✔**MUSEUM OF FLIGHT, nr HADDINGTON:** 01620 880308.
D1 3km from A1 NE of town. In the old complex of hangars and nis-sen huts at the side of E Fortune, an airfield dating to World War I, a large collection of planes from gliders to jets and esp wartime memorabilia respectfully restored and preserved. Inspired and inspiring displays; not just boys' stuff. Marvel at the bravery back then and sense the unremit-ting passage of time. From E Fortune the airship R34 made its historic Atlantic crossings. Apr-Oct 7 days, 10.30am-5pm (until 6pm Jul and Aug).

488 ✔**DOUGAL PHILIP'S GARDEN CENTRE, nr SOUTH QUEENSFERRY:**
B1 01506 834433. On A904 S Queensferry to Bo'ness/Linlithgow rd 6km from Forth Br t/off on M90. Relocated from the famous walled garden of Hopetoun House, so more convenient if less ambient. Nevertheless, best selection of garden plants around. This is where Edinburgh's discerning gardeners come to potter. 7 days, 10am-5.30pm.

489 **GLENKINCHIE DISTILLERY (TOUR), PENCAITLAND:** 01875 342004.
D2 Only 25km from the city centre (via A68 and A6093 before Pathhead), so popular. Founded in 1837 in a peaceful, pastoral place (it's 3km from the village) with its own bowling green; a country trip as well as a whisky tour. They have occasional 'silent seasons', so check since all you'd see then is a video. State-of-the art visitor centre opened 1996. May-Sep tours daily until 4pm, Oct-Mar Mon-Fri until 4pm.

490 **ROOM AT THE TOP, BATHGATE:** 01506 635707. Menzies Rd. You can
A2 spend half an hr driving around the centre of Bathgate before you twig that the huge thing next to Safeway is a purpose-built nightclub – the UK's biggest. (Cream and Ministry of Sound come on down!) Proprietor doesn't like the word superclub, hyperbole wouldn't do it justice. Capacity of 2600, more dance floors, bars, nooks and (snogging) crannies than you can use.

491 **SAM BURN'S YARD, PRESTONPANS:** 01875 810600. On the coast rd
C1 out of Musselburgh; if you get to Prestonpans you've missed it. By a gate in the wall you'll see cars on the kerb on a long straight stretch. The yard has piles of old bikes, assorted 'stuff' and is full of domestic and office fur-niture stored both outdoors and in sheds. Popular with Sun browsers, although you wonder who might want a rusted filing cabinet or a sec-ond-hand toilet. 7 days till 5pm, Sun from 12.30pm.

SMEATON GARDENS, EAST LINTON: Report: 455/WOODLAND WALKS.

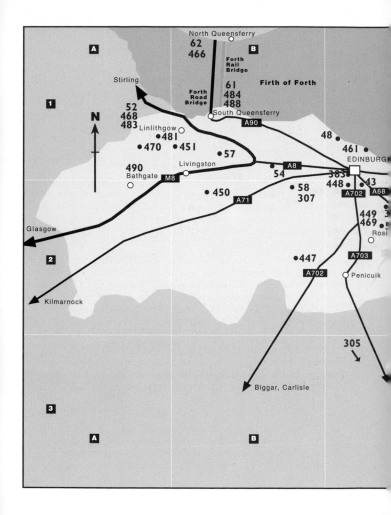

North Queensferry
62
466

B

A

Forth
Rail
Bridge

61
484
488

Firth of Forth

Stirling

52
468
483 Linlithgow
• **481**
• **470** • **451**
• **57**

Forth
Road
Bridge

South Queensferry

A90

48 •
461 •
EDINBURGH

1

N

Livingston

54
A8

383 • **43**
448 **A702** **A68**

490
Bathgate

M8

• **450**

A71

• **58**
307

449
469 •
Rosl

2

Glasgow

• **447**

A703

A702
Penicuik

Kilmarnock

305

3

Biggar, Carlisle

A

B

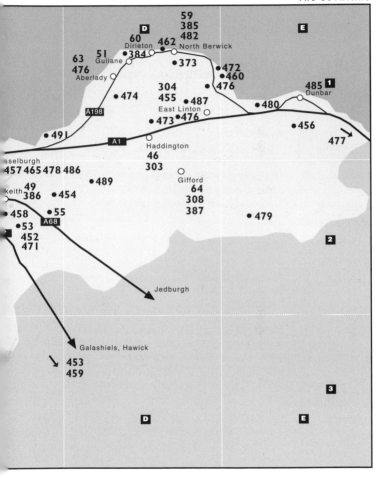

59
385
482

D

60
Dirleton   462
Gullane   384   North Berwick
51

63
476
Aberlady

E

373

472
460
476

304
474   455   487
East Linton
473 476

485 **1**
Dunbar

480

491

456
477

A198

A1

Haddington
46
303

sselburgh
457 465 478 486

Gifford
64
308
387

Keith
49
386   454   489

458
55
53   A68
452
471

479

2

Jedburgh

Galashiels, Hawick

453
459

D

E

3

117

THE VERY BEST SHOPS

These are the shops that get it right. Edinburghers in the know go here.

FOOD AND DRINK

BAKERS

Bread **JENNER'S**, Princes St. 225 2442. Only Edin stockist of Fisher and Donaldson's Dr Floyd's bread.
AULD ALLIANCE, 32 Victoria St. 622 7080.

Bread/Italian **VALVONA & CROLLA**, 19 Elm Row. 556 6066.

Custard Pies **IRVINE'S**, 16 Clerk St. 667 0262.

Italian **FRANCHINO'S PASTICCERIA**, 14 Albert St. 554 7417.
ANGELO'S, 20a Brougham Pl.

Pâtisserie **FLORENTIN**, 8 St Giles St. 225 6267.

BUTCHERS

Free Range **GEORGE BOWER**, 75 Raeburn Pl. 332 3469.

DELICATESSEN

General **GLASS & THOMPSON**, 2 Dundas St. 557 0909.
VALVONA & CROLLA, 19 Elm Row. 556 6066.
PECKHAM'S, 159 Bruntsfield Pl. 229 7054. Also at Waverley Stn.

Cheese **IAIN MELLIS**, 30a Victoria St. 226 6215. Also at 205 Bruntsfield Pl. 447 7414. Also has deli produce and fruit 'n' veg.
HERBIE, 66 Raeburn Pl. 332 9888. Esp brie.

Mexican **LUPE PINTO'S**, 24 Leven St, Bruntsfield. 228 6241.

FISHMONGERS

General **GEORGE ARMSTRONG**, 80 Raeburn Pl. 315 2033. Also at The Gyle Shopping Centre, way out West.
CLARK BROS, 2 Harbour New St, Musselburgh. 665 6181.
LONGA FISH, 23 Leven St, Tollcross. 229 2160.
SOMETHING FISHY, 16a Broughton St. 556 7614.

Seafood **TSE'S FISH MARKET**, 2 Warrender Park Rd. 229 4207.

FRUIT AND VEG

General **FARMER JACK'S**, 5 Graham St. 553 6090.
VALVONA & CROLLA, 19 Elm Row. 556 6066. Produce fresh from Milan.
ARGYLE PL. There are several shops selling fresh produce in this st.

Organic **REAL FOODS**, 37 Broughton St. 557 1911. Also at 8 Broughton St. 228 1201.
ORGANIC FOOD SHOP, 47 Broughton St. 556 1772.

HAGGIS **MACSWEEN'S FACTORY**, Dryden Rd, Bilston Glen, Loanhead. 10 km S of the city centre. 440 2555.

ICE CREAM **LUCA'S**, 34 High St, Musselburgh. 665 2237. Also at 16 Morningside Rd. 446 6233.

LATE-NIGHT **ALLDAYS**. 24 hr general stores at Nicholson St, Raeburn Pl and Leith Walk.
COSTCUTTER. 24 hr general store at Lothian Rd.
SAINSBURY'S, Blackhall. 332 0704. Supermarket open 24 hrs on Fri night.

ORIENTAL GROCERS **PAT'S CHUNG YING CHINESE SUPERMARKET**, 199 Leith Walk. 554 0358.
SIN FUNG, 16 Bruntsfield Pl. 228 6007.

PASTA **GOURMET PASTA**, 52 Morningside Rd. 447 4750.

SWEETS **CASEY JAMES**, 52 St Mary's St. 556 6082.

WHOLEFOODS **REAL FOODS**, 37 Broughton St. 557 1911. Also at 8 Brougham St. 228 1201.
ROOTS, 60 Newington Rd. 668 2888.

WINE AND BEER **J.E. HOGG**, 61 Cumberland St. 556 4025.
IRVINE ROBERTSON WINES, 10 N Leith Sands. 553 3521.
PETER GREEN, 37a/b Warrender Park Rd. 229 5925.
OASTS & TOASTS, 107–09 Morrison St. 228 8088.

The Very Best Shops

HOUSE AND HOME

DEPARTMENT STORES	**JENNER'S**, Princes St. 225 2442. **JOHN LEWIS**, St James Centre. 556 9121.
IRONMONGERS	**GRAYS**, 89 George St. 225 7381.
FLOWERS	**RAEBURN GROCERS**, 23 Comely Bank Rd. 332 5166. **FLOWERS BY MAXWELL**, 32 Castle St. 226 2866. **NARCISSUS**, 50a Broughton St. 478 7447. **STEMS**, 24 Grindlay St. 228 5575.
BEDDING	**AND SO TO BED**, 22 Howe St. 225 6998.
BRUSHES	**ROBERT CHESSER**, 40 Victoria St. 225 2181.
CERAMICS	**WARE ON EARTH**, 15 Howe St. 558 1276. **AZTECA**, 5 Grassmarket. 229 9368.
FURNITURE American	**THE GREAT AMERICAN INDOORS**, 10 Springvalley Grds. 447 5795.
Modern	**INHOUSE**, 28 Howe St. 225 2888.
Traditional	**SHAPES**, 1–3 Bankhead Medway. 453 3222.
RUGS	**ORIENTAL RUGS OF DISTINCTION**, 297 Canongate. 556 6952. **WHYTOCK & REID**, Belford Mews. 226 4911.
TILES	**THE ORIGINAL TILE COMPANY**, 23a Howe St. 556 2013. **EDINBURGH CERAMICS**, 46 Balcarres St. 452 8145.

CLOTHES AND APPEARANCE

BARBERS	**WOODS**, 12 Drummond St. 556 6716.
HAIRDRESSERS	**CHEYNES**, 45 York Pl. 558 1010. Also at 3 Drumsheugh Pl. 225 2234.

LUGGAGE AND BAGS	**CHARLIE MILLER**, 13 Stafford St. 226 5550.
	A.D. MACKENZIE, 34 Victoria St. 220 0089.

MEN'S CLOTHES

New Labels
CRUISE, St Mary's St. 556 2532. Also at 94 George St. 226 3524. Giorgio, Hugo, Ralph, Hughie.
SMITHS, 124 High St. 225 5927.

Established Labels
AUSTIN REED, 39 George St. 225 6703

Both
JENNER'S, Princes St. 225 2442.
HOUSE OF FRASER, 145 Princes St. 225 2472.

Old Clothes
PADDIE BARRASS, 15 Grassmarket. 226 3087.
ELAINE'S, 53 St Stephen St.
FLIP, 60 S Br. 556 4966.

Outdoor Clothes
GRAHAM TISO, 13 Wellington Pl. 554 0804. Also at Rose St. 225 9486.

RUDE STUFF
LEATHER & LACE, 8 Drummond St. 557 9413.
WHIPLASH TRASH, 53 Cockburn St. 226 1005.

SHOES

Shoes that Last
BARNET'S, 7 High St. 556 3577.

Modish
SCHUH, 32 N Br. 225 6552. Also at 6 Frederick St. 220 0290.

SPORTS

General
MACKENZIE'S, 17 Nicholson St. 667 2288.
AITKEN AND NIVEN, 77–79 George St. 225 1461.

Snowboarding
WHITE STUFF, Hanover St. 624 2424.
BOARDWISE, 4–8 Lady Lawson St. 229 5887.

Surfing
MOMENTUM, 22 Bruntsfield Pl. 229 6665.

WOMEN'S CLOTHES

New Labels
CRUISE, 9 St Mary's St. 556 2532.
STUFF, 94 George St. 226 3524.
CORNICHE, 2 Jeffrey St. 556 3707.
JANE DAVIDSON, 152 Thistle St. 225 3280.

Posh Frock Hire
DRESS HIRE STUDIO, 19 Grassmarket. 225 7391.

The Very Best Shops

Woolies	**JUDITH GLUE**, 64 High St. 556 5443.
	NUMBER TWO, St Stephen Pl. 225 6257.
	BILL BABER, 66 Grassmarket. 225 3249.
	THE CASHMERE STORE, 2 St Giles St. 225 4055.
	HILLARY ROHDE, 332 4147 (exclusive cashmere by appointment only).

MISCELLANEOUS

ANTIQUES	
General	Grassmarket, Victoria St, Thistle St, St Stephen St and NW Circus Pl all have shops selling a wide range of antiques.
Bric-a-brac	**BYZANTIUM**, 9 Victoria St. 225 1768.
	UNICORN, 65 Dundas St. 556 7176.
Clothes	**HAND IN HAND**, 3 NW Circus Pl. 226 3598.
Jewellery	**JOSEPH BONNAR**, 72 Thistle St. 226 2811.
CARDS	
General	**PAPER TIGER**, Stafford St. 226 5812. Also at 53 Lothian Rd. 228 2790.
Funniest	**PJ'S**, 60 Broughton St.
Playing/Tarot	**SOMERVILLE'S**, 82 Canongate. 556 5225.
COMICS	**DEAD HEAD COMICS**, 27 Candlemaker Row. 226 2774.
	FORBIDDEN PLANET, 40–41 S Br. 558 8226.
COOKBOOKS	**CLARISSA DICKSON-WRIGHT'S COOK BOOKSHOP** Grassmarket. 226 4445.
JOKES	**AHA HA HA**, 99 W Bow. 220 5252.
JUNK	**EASY**, Couper St, Leith. 554 7077.
	JUST JUNK, Broughton St. 557 4385.
	SAM BURNS' YARD, main rd to Prestonpans, 25 km from Edin.
	UTILITIES, Broughton St.
LATE CHEMIST	**BOOTS**, 48 Shandwick Pl. 225 6757. Open till 9pm.

MODELS	**MARIONVILLE MODELS**, 42 Turnhouse Rd. 317 7010. **MAC'S MODELS**, 168 Canongate. 557 5551. **WONDERLAND**, 397 Lothian Rd. 229 6428.
NEWSPAPERS	**INTERNATIONAL NEWSAGENTS**, 367 High St. 225 4827.
PRESENTS	**ROUND THE WORLD**, 82 W Bow. 225 7086. Also at NW Circus Pl. 225 7800. **OUT OF THE NOMAD'S TENT**, St Leonard's Lane. 662 1612. **STUDIO ONE**, 10 Stafford St. 226 5812. **BLACKADDER GALLERY**, 5 Raeburn Pl. 332 4605. **GALERIE MIRAGES**, 46a Raeburn Pl. 315 2603.
TOBACCO	**THE PIPE SHOP**, 92 Leith Walk. 553 3561.
SOUVENIRS	See below and **ANYWHERE ON THE HIGH ST**.
TARTAN AND SERIOUS	**KINLOCH ANDERSON**, Commercial St. 555 1355. **HECTOR RUSSELL**, Princes St. 225 3315. Also at High St. 558 1254.
TARTAN AND TACKY	Not hard to find.
VIDEO RENTAL	**ALPHABET VIDEO**, 22 Marchmont Rd. 229 5136. **C & A VIDEO**, 93 Broughton St. 556 1866.

BORTHWICK CASTLE 'this magnificent tower house knocks you off your horse with its authenticity' (page 25)

INDEX

125

Index

Other Collins Scottish Titles

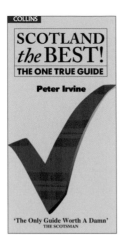

Scotland the Best!
(ISBN 0 00 472399-6, priced £12.99)

Glasgow the Best!
(ISBN 0 00 472465-8, priced £6.99)

Edinburgh Step by Step
(ISBN 0 00 472346-5, priced £6.99)